TRIALS AND TRIUMPHS OF

DIMINISHMENT

Great grace
to you,
Joy Brewster

I think you may find this
reading as delightful as I did!
Thank God that our paths
keep crossing, one way & another!!

George Brewster

TRIALS AND TRIUMPHS OF

DIMINISHMENT

A MEMOIR

JOY BREWSTER

CLEMENTS PUBLISHING
Toronto

Published 2011 by Clements Publishing Group Inc.
6021 Yonge Street, Box 213
Toronto, Ontario M2M 3W2 Canada
www.clementspublishing.com

Unless otherwise noted, all Scripture quotations are from the
HOLY BIBLE, NEW INTERNATIONAL VERSION
copyright © 1973, 1978, 1984 by the International Bible Society.

Library and Archives Canada Cataloguing in Publication

Brewster, Joy, 1932–
Trials and Triumphs of Diminishment : a memoir /
Joy Brewster.

ISBN 978-1-894667-88-3

1. Brewster, Joy, 1932-. 2. Aging—Religious aspects—Christianity.
3. Death—Religious aspects—Christianity.
4. Christian life. 5. Christian biography—Canada. I. Title.

BR1725.B74A3 2011   248.4   C2010-907394-0

To all those who prayed for me, who joined with God
to bring me THROUGH

ACKNOWLEDGMENTS

My immense gratitude to the following:

To my prayer partners, Cheryl Buchanan and Lynda Kinnee for your faithfulness in listening, counseling, encouraging, and never failing prayer for me.

To my "trial" readers who responded with enthusiasm, encouragement, and good counsel after reading the manuscript: Anna Beketov, who edited and gave great wisdom, support, and encouragement, Lynda MacDonald, Bill MacDonald, Ruth Hall, Susan Chambers, Marita Judson, Colleen Sumners, Linda Hicks, George Brewster, Cheryl Buchanan, Lynda Kinnee, and my dear sister, Rose, who was and is a constant encouragement to me.

To my pastor, Mark Buchanan, who took time in his packed schedule to read my manuscript and to give me sound advice regarding it.

To my husband, George, for his never failing love and encouragement, and support. Thank you—all of you—who prayed for me faithfully and persistently. My church family, New Life Baptist in Duncan, you are incredible. I especially thank the friends in California, as well as those of my childhood in Pleasant Grove, especially Mildred Kemp and Gina King. Your gift of love through prayer had tremendous effect.

To my Oregon friends of a lifetime, Rebecca and Ann; you always cheer my heart.

CONTENTS

PART THREE: VISTAS OF JOY

INTRODUCTION

Why would anyone write a memoir mainly about loss? Many good instructional books have been written on grief and loss, and this is not one of them. There is a strong downside to what I have experienced, but there is also an unexpected upside that encouraged me, and I pray may encourage others.

I began writing this memoir because I felt a strong compelling to do so. I knew I hadn't had the worst experience of diminishment—not at all when compared to others I have known. Yet my experience was impacting enough to change my life profoundly. It brought me into such a new realm of living and learning and focus that I felt I must record it.

Perhaps I have given too many details of my own life so that there is too much emphasis on me. Yet I could only draw from what was happening to me, and therefore I felt the need to make it clear. Also I did not record the similar experiences of others because I didn't know what their experiences had produced, and I hadn't and still do not have the energy to research theirs.

No, this is merely my memoir, recording what my experience brought to me. I do not say others will learn the same things I did, but I believe many will struggle with the same issues, and I offer my experiences and insights just as they are for me, and without the intent to draw conclusions about others.

My sincere desire is to glorify God by revealing his amazing grace to me. I also desire to draw readers to a better understanding of diminishment, both the losses and resulting grief and also the richness of new learning and experiencing it brings.

PART I:

THE NARROWING ROAD

Do not cast me away when I am old
do not forsake me when my
strength is gone.
Psalm 71:9

Teach us to number our days
aright
that we may gain a heart wisdom.
Psalm 90:12

It was good for me to be afflicted
so that I might learn your decrees.
Psalm 119:71

CHAPTER ONE

THE FALL

That day in early May 2007, is indelible in my mind. That was the day everything changed for me. I didn't grow old gracefully; I was dumped into it.

I knew I would be having my seventy-fifth birthday in October, but I just couldn't get in touch with my age. I felt no older than sixty certainly and in many ways younger. Oh, I knew there were signs of age and a lessening of energy as the years passed. There was no mistaking the cracking sound of bending, lines on the face, sagging skin. I had slowed down and scheduled less, gradually, for at least a decade. I could no longer do the hill climbing I had loved so much, and I no longer ran up stairs two at a time. But all in all I was healthy, fit, active and could still manage to move with agility on level ground. Blessed—that's what I was. I was careful to have yearly physical examinations, always to be told I was in great shape. Only minor problems brought me to my doctor and that infrequently as the years passed. Currently I was unaware of any medical problems that were incapacitating and figured that my slightly high blood pressure was just par for the course. Brimming with health and energy, I thought.

That May morning I walked the river path in glad stride, drinking in the sunshine and the beauty of the day. This walk was a daily treat for me, an earth child, outdoor girl, nature lover, and I took it each day I could, as early as possible. The woods and river invited my "walk and talk" time with God; our fellowship was rich as I admired his handiwork with him before launching the day. "Bless the Lord, O my soul/ And forget none of his benefits"—mine were many indeed: George, my husband; my children Glen and Karen, and grandchildren, Josh and Krystal, teenagers now, in California; my dear sister, Rose and my brothers Jerry and Barry and all my big Texas family; my incredible church family here in Duncan, B.C., my joyous staff ministry at New Life Church as Director of Counseling Ministries, and my service as Elder of the church; my many friends and neighbors; a large comfortable house, two cars and a travel van, no money problems, all bills paid, interesting travels and vacations. The list went on and on. My heart sang praise.

And nature. I was ever the lover of beauty, and for me God's creation was always new and fresh. The tall trees, grasses, vines, and flowers drew me in to serene joy. I found it wonderful to live by this river, to see its flow and shine each day, to meditate and pray by its waters. This day I lingered by each view site, praying, listening, praising.

As I walked along, the path diverged away from the river; now for views I had to walk small trails leading to the river side. One especially intrigued me, and I decided abruptly to follow it (Adventure is my middle name)—I was ever one to follow an urge to explore, however small. I left the main path, impulsively seeking to follow the narrow trail, forgetting my dialog with God. Coming to a small stream, I found it too wide to leap, but I noticed that I could cross it by a log that had fallen or been placed across it. Hesitating for only a moment to give it a try, I suddenly felt sure footed enough to make it and decided to go on. I tentatively tried it with my foot; it felt a bit slick, but not a problem—I tip-toed across with no trouble, agile as a ballet dancer. My smile spread with triumph. Down to the river then, I stood mesmerized, relishing the peaceful flow of the water, the beauty of the trees and sky. Then I turned back.

At the log I didn't pause but stepped right on, sure of my agility. That was the moment. My foot slipped suddenly! I felt myself begin to slide. Quick fear's adrenalin shot through me. Jerking back to right myself, I slipped further, lost control, and plunged abruptly down into the frigid water of the small stream. I lurched in off balance, legs first, plunged into icy water, then, twisted and mired in the soft bottom, I fell forward onto my knees, twisting my back and flailing my arms as I fell, finally settling onto my hands and knees, face inches above the muddy water. Pain shot through me; I didn't move.

Shocked and stunned, I tried to register reality. It had all happened in seconds. I stayed put as the pain subsided and as I assessed my situation. Emotion rushed in: I felt immeasurably embarrassed at my sodden state and very foolish that I had been so cock-sure of myself. Gazing around, I hoped fervently that no one had seen the spectacle. Immediately I called on God, confessing stupidity: "Pride goeth before a fall." I asked for mercy and voiced a plea that I had not injured myself badly. Slowly I dragged myself out of the water and took inventory. I knew I had wrenched my knees, and I felt the pain, but I found I could still walk well enough if I shortened my steps. So, shuffling along like a rained on bag lady, hair straggling down, water dripping off my mud-stained clothes, I began making my way home, hoping, hoping I wouldn't encounter anyone on the way.

Amazingly I didn't. All the way I muttered my stupidity to God, repeatedly confessed my pride, and asked for mercy. I knew he knew all, but I poured it out anyway. Finally I neared the house. As quickly as I could, I made my way through the garage and into my bathroom, stripping for a hot shower and fresh clothes, quietly so George wouldn't hear. Avoiding more embarrassment and any probing questions, I said nothing to him about it at the time. I dressed rather awkwardly, took two Tylenol, said a swift good-bye to my husband, leaving him no time for a closer look, and drove to my counseling appointments at the church.

By this time, I was feeling little discomfort except for the considerable stiffness and pain in my knees, and though I knew they were swelling, I kept telling myself that I wasn't hurt badly. I decided to go ahead with my day and deal with my knees after my two appointments. I trudged up the path to the church office wing slowly but with determination. It helped me with my self-deception as I told myself again that this whole incident was "not too bad."

I made it into my office, took my seat, and called out my welcome to my counselees sitting down. After finishing both my appointments, I could hardly get out of my chair. I stood precariously and tried a few unsteady steps. O.K., I could make it. With my careful, mincing walk out of my office, I waved good-bye to the secretary. But she saw my plight and immediately secured for me a wheelchair and a ride to my car. There I stood, moving very slowly, yet inside feeling tense and urgent and longing to hurry, for I knew I needed to get home before I couldn't get into my car and maneuver enough to drive. Seating myself sideways on the driver's seat and then grasping and moving in each leg, I swiveled and wedged my swollen knees under the steering wheel, and painfully and carefully began to drive. When I reached home I stole into the house, then stripped down to view my now grossly swollen knees. This was serious. I had to face it. I drew a deep breath, asked God again for mercy, and reluctantly called George to hear my confession, pouring out my story without eye contact. I finished by asking him to take me to Emergency. By this time I felt utterly foolish and terribly embarrassed. Silently I berated myself, "Stupid, stupid, stupid!" George, loving as he is, did not scold or berate, but I knew he hurt to see my pain and embarrassment; he helped me into the car and drove me quickly to the hospital.

The doctor at Emergency who examined me found I had bad sprains, but no breaks that he could detect. He ordered x-rays of my back—there was now some pain there too—as well as knees and legs. I had these taken and then went home to go to bed and to continued pain, in spite of Tylenol 3. By this time I needed crutches, though I had none at the time, and had difficulty rolling myself into bed. Sleep didn't come easily as I had hoped it would. Staring at the darkness that night, I told God again what a fool I'd been and thanked him for getting me through the day.

But this was just the beginning.

The next day my family doctor called about the X-rays: I had suffered a spinal compression and had two hair-line fractures in my vertebrae and one on the top of my leg bone. How's that for "not too bad"? Nothing was required, he assured me, except carefulness, minimal activity, and lots of rest. "And for heaven's sake, don't fall whatever you do!" he added. I hung up in something of a stupor, unable to take it all in. What had I done to myself?

Summer was now beginning, so I reduced my schedule at church as I usually did in the summer months, and began to spend much time with my feet elevated. All my lovely walks along the river were over for a time, but to sit among the flowers and trees in the back yard gave me some consolation. By mid summer I was on my feet again and moving about well, and thankful. But one thing didn't return—my energy.

In spite of my light schedule, August found me flagged and without stamina.

I also began having severe blood pressure problems, headaches, and increased lethargy. My doctor ordered more tests. By this time doing anything requiring strength and concentration proved difficult for me, even light household chores and cooking. Sleep was what I craved, night and day.

Finally, in September my family doctor told me the latest test results showed I had a problem with my kidneys; they were not filtering protein to a large measure, and were just passing it on out. It was not getting into my system as it should. My doctor referred me to a kidney specialist. But I soon learned I would have to wait weeks to see this busy specialist, and wait I did.

All through the remainder of late summer I waited, hopeful that my physical condition would improve and I would be back to my full schedule of ministry and activities by the fall, and I planned accordingly. By the middle of September, I was forced to face the truth: I had near zero energy, pure and simple. I felt immensely tired, both body and brain. My schedule would need to be greatly reduced if I was to work at all. But by the end of September, I knew I had no choice—I had to come to a full stop. This was a devastating realization. I prayed fervently to be restored, to be healed. Instead I grew weaker. God's will was clear: I had to stop everything—staff, eldership, counseling, the class I had planned to teach. All. There was no other option. Full stop. I cried, berated myself, lamented my losses, and prayed they were temporary. But stop I must.

So I did. I resigned sorrowfully from each ministry, and now spent much of my time in bed. My weakness was now so great I felt what

I thought someone ninety years old would experience. It seemed I had jumped three decades in three months. Shock, dismay, and fear consumed me. What was happening to me? How serious was it?

Wonderful church friends rallied to meet our needs, praying, bringing meals (Scotty and Beth Cook especially were "food angels" bringing meal after meal), offering help of any and all kinds.

I called the kidney specialist's office. No, he would not be able to see me any time soon. His schedule was totally full, his office assistant told me; he would see me when he could. I waited.

Meanwhile my weakness continued. My birthday month of October was the worst of my life up to that time in terms of my physical well-being. I was receiving no treatment, and I had no idea whether my condition was life-threatening or not.

Finally I was called for an appointment with the specialist on October 29. After his examination, he told me I had nephritis, inflammation of the kidneys. He drew it out for me, making it as clear as he could. He also informed me that there are fifty kinds of nephritis, and that I needed a kidney biopsy to determine the exact kind I had. No treatment could be prescribed until this was determined. Again a three week wait. I was too tired to cry, but not too tired to be utterly depressed.

I asked how I had developed this condition, but he said he could not answer that. It is, he said, usually hereditary. That made sense: my mother had had kidney problems for years before her death, and my maternal grandfather had died of kidney failure. But I couldn't help wondering if my fall had brought this on. Had I done this to myself? No one knew.

Then on November 20 I had the biopsy and by the end of November, the specialist gave me a full accounting of my problems and a strong array of medications to treat it, mainly prednisone and cyclosporine, both of which have strong side effects.

He prescribed various other medications to treat the side effects. All in all, he prescribed eleven pills to take each day, some of them twice a day.

I felt a new fear; I was alarmed about taking all these substances into my body.

I had rarely needed medicines of any kind. What permanent effects would I experience from these? How much swelling would I get from the prednisone? How much weight gain? How much pain and discomfort from the side effects? Would I even know myself? Did I have a choice? The specialist pointed out that if I didn't try the medicines, I would have to go straight to dialysis. He advised the medical route, hoping for a cure.

I prayed fervently that I would make the right choice. Others prayed too.

At length I decided, in fear and trembling, to take the medicines. After a few days, just as the instruction sheets warned, I had abundant sleep disturbances, weight gain, great fatigue and weariness, mood changes, and digestive upsets. Poor me! Poor George! But I adjusted to it, or endured it, praying for improvement in my condition. Eventually I did improve to an extent for a few months.

Yet the three months leading up to and the months of treatment that followed were extraordinary. They brought me time to reflect and think, and so produced some of the greatest learning of my life. I do not want ever to forget what insights I believe the Lord gave me in those days. I faced some of the greatest questions of my life, and I received answers to them, not always as fully as I might want, but in some cases with a fullness that was surprising and very helpful. My continued experience brought further insights. Later new trials and even greater problems arose to try my learning in this lab of experience. So I record my learning now, lest I forget what I believe has been shown me by the Holy Spirit, about walking the road of diminishment, the last mile of my life.

In each chapter I have sought to reveal what the Lord revealed to me, that for every trial, all debilitation of illness and diminishment of old age, he gives an exchange of blessing—but blessing not easily seen nor apprehended unless I am listening closely to what he is teaching me.

As I have progressed in the writing of Part I, I have come to realize that the topics I have presented are related and interrelated. Yet each seems worthy of examination. So at the risk of repeating myself, I have attempted to give a chapter to each area of focus. In each I have found the manifold and searing sorrows of loss, yet deepening fellowship with the Triune God, along with awesome and surprising learning on this last mile home. In Part II I continue with my journey through my deepest valley of the shadow. In Part III I reveal how I have come to live daily in diminishment.

Make no mistake: diminishment hurts. The losses are many, the hurts deep, and grief prevails. Yet there is a counter-side, and that is what I asked God that I might see clearly and understand.

"Therefore we do not lose heart. Though outwardly we are wasting away, yet inwardly we are being renewed day by day. For our light and momentary troubles are achieving for us an eternal glory that far outweighs them all. So we fix our eyes not on what is seen, but on what is unseen. For what is seen is temporal, but what is unseen is eternal." (2 Corinthians 4:16–17)

CHAPTER TWO

FACING THE FEAR

When I was five years old, I lived with my young parents and brother, Jerry, a year and nine months older than I, in a four room house, minus electricity, indoor plumbing, and insulation, on the edge of prairie farmland. But we could see the shining Dallas skyline nine miles away, rising in splendor above the flat lands surrounding it. My father traveled there almost daily, driving over the Trinity River bed, to whatever job he was able to hold, usually welding.

I had little idea how very poor we were; everyone in our small community seemed equally as poor. It was 1937. During it and all the Depression years, all those in my community wore hand-me-downs and no shoes except Sundays, all ate mainly vegetables from the garden and drank milk from the cow. All lived in tiny houses warmed by wood-burning stoves, pot bellied or cook stoves, or small room gas heaters.

All drove ancient cars, or rode bikes, or walked to church, store, school, and to visit one another. All worried about money, food, and fuel. Most prayed through and worked hard wherever they could.

There was never an end to the worries of my mother, expressed by her frequent sighs and tears and occasional cries of anguish or frustration, and of my father's frowns and scowls and temper outbursts. They didn't mean to infect their children with their fears, but in my quietness I learned a steady and growing tightness of belly, a careful hiding, a seeking out of places to feel safe, and found it only now and then as I sought safe haven in my mother's arms, or in my dad's lap.

Not that there was often time for such. Always more needed to be done. But evenings we all welcomed the radio programs and the entertainment they brought. We laughed at Jack Benny or Bob Hope, or we listened to country western music, and in season we went to sleep to the sound of the nightly baseball broadcast. While we sat around the radio, I managed to snag a lap now and then and snuggle into safety.

Added to daily worries came the threat of war in Europe. Three of my father's siblings and their spouses and children lived near by and visited often. When they did, the evening might feature a mound of home-grown pop-corn, piled high in a small wash tub, and laugh laden games of dominoes in the corner of the kitchen. But as the thirties edged towards the forties I would tuck myself in a corner of our tiny living room, listening to their anxious talk of Hitler and his plans for Europe. Blitzkrieg. The fall of Paris. The bombing of London. When would it reach us? Would my daddy have to go fight? What would become of us?

My fear grew and spread, but I held it inside with a careful silence, though its threats invaded my dreams. I was a great embarrassment to myself with my bed-wetting. Fear was not a word I used for what I felt, but I know it was a constant underlying presence. As I grew, I came to realize my fear and to experience its surfacing many times unmistakably. The hidden pocket of it in my inner being never quite emptied.

Before I received a full diagnosis and treatment for the nephritis, I was in limbo. I really had no definitive word on how severe my condition was. And my blood pressure was sky-rocketing. My family doctor tried many ways to bring it down, but it took a long time to do so. While it was still high, I greatly feared a stroke. One night I was wracked with a migraine headache so severe and with such high blood pressure readings that I finally asked George to take me to Emergency. That night more than any other I faced the greatest fear of my life—that I might die. I could not remember ever being so afraid; every cell in me registered it.

My immense fear surprised me. I had been raised by Christian parents and in the church. I know they worried about a lot of things, but death wasn't one of them. I had never thought I would be afraid of death. With faith in the resurrection of Christ, I fully believed that when I died I would be taken to heaven where a glorious life awaited me. Well acquainted with the scriptures concerning life after death, I had often quoted them to many. I especially loved to dwell on Paul's words in Philippians, "If I am to go on living in the body, this will mean fruitful labor for me. Yet what shall I choose? I do not know! I am torn between the two: I desire to depart and be with Christ, which is better by far" (Philippians 1: 22–23). I believed that the moment I died I would go to heaven to be with Christ, entering into an eternal existence far better than life I had known on earth. I truly believed. Why then was I so afraid?

It amazed me that I had never seriously contemplated my own death. I could not understand how this could be so. Had I no near misses in my life?

My mind flashed to that day of my near drowning. Seventeen, a cocky high school senior, I was delivering our school paper to advertisers along with Janice, a fellow "reporter" on the school newspaper staff. Looking for a lark, we had begged Jimmy for the loan of his old car, grabbed a stack of papers, and set out in the rain. I soon discovered as I drove that if I applied the brakes, the car pulled sharply to the right, and I quickly made correction. I noted the fact but without apprehension and went back to my talking and laughing with Janice. On the downside of a rise, I automatically applied the brakes, but this time there was no time to correct. I hit mud. The car shot off the road like the firing of a cannon, flying out over a large pond at the bottom of the hill. In horror, we sailed an incredible moment through the air. Then the car smacked into the pond, sinking immediately as the water poured in the open windows. In that split second, Janice dove out her window above the water flow—she was moving out the instant the car hit.

But I was fastened too tightly under the steering wheel, deluged by the flood that pummeled me. In panic I fought to move but could not. Terrified, I realized I might not be able to wait for the car to settle so I could swim out. Now I totally feared I was going to drown. And die! I was going to die!

That moment I became aware of an inner voice counseling me to be calm, to hold my breath, to wait until the flood subsided. My panic ended; I did exactly as instructed and within a few moments I scrambled and wedged myself out through the window and swam clumsily, dragging along in my stylish heavy skirt and petticoats and heavy shoes to the nearby shore. I screamed in hysteria when I reached it, but I was safe! That was the one time I remembered that I had actually believed I might die.

Beyond that I couldn't remember a time I had felt that my actual life was in danger of ending. Not in the small sailboat on Lake Erie, heading for a crash against the massive breakwater, not on the side of a cliff I was trying to scale when I slipped, not on the rainiest night of our lives (which turned out to be a tornado) when I drove my sister and myself home from Austin to Dallas. Torrents of rain slashed us horizontally. Then a monstrous truck barreled down on us, driving us right off the road. Near misses to be sure, and incredibly frightening. Each left me weak with fright, but somehow none had made me fear that I would actually die. Suffer, oh yes, but surely not die.

I think as the years passed I made an assumption—and now I realize I am a person given to assumptions—that I would live to a grand old age, weaken quickly, and die peacefully. Not a logical or even a reasonable conclusion, yet present because of my good health and escapes from near misses.

So why was I absolutely terrified this night in Emergency? Clearly I was fearing death. I felt this all encompassing fear in my entire body, and especially in my stomach and muscles, knotted, tense, gnawing. I was that little girl again, lying curled in her bed, overwhelmed by terror. Now, though I asked that God would take it away and sought to rest myself in him, it grasped me like manacles of iron. "Why?" I asked the Lord, "why am I in this jail of fear?" I heard only the loud voice of my terror. In the midst of it all, I felt ashamed, without faith, a spiritual bed-wetter.

Mustering my will and focus, I diligently recalled what I knew. I believed that death would have no victory and that heaven would be fantastic. I would see the Lord. What joy that would be! I knew I truly and earnestly believed and had joyfully shared these beliefs with others. Yet that night it made no difference; my terror continued, and though surprised by it, I could neither dispel it nor even diminish it with all my recalling my beliefs and remembering scriptures.

My head believed. My emotions told a different story, and my body responded. In my pride I shared my fears with no one, having practiced silence all my life, and grew tighter inside, trying to escape, trying to hide. These life-long habits just served, I think, to magnify my fear and my shame.

At Emergency, I was given shots of morphine, and at last I slept. The pain ebbed; the terror subsided in forced sleep. I came home the next morning relieved of pain. But I had little relief from my fear; it emerged again and asserted itself in the familiar ways. For days I remained largely in this tormenting state. I pressed myself on the Lord; I sought his lap; I questioned him repeatedly and sought to listen for his voice for help. Finally, with no stroke happening, I grew calm enough to reclaim his presence, to rest myself in him, and then to *hear* him and to receive the true comfort I so desperately needed.

These thoughts came: some resistance of death is inevitable, for though we know some wonderful things about heaven, it is largely unknowable in its fullness until we actually arrive. We have beautiful descriptions in Revelation, but can any one of us say for certain that he or she can visualize these with accuracy? Paul tells us:

> However, as it is written:
> "No eye has seen
> no ear has heard
> no mind has conceived
> what God has prepared for those who love him—"
> but God has revealed it to us by his Spirit. (1 Corinthians 2:9–10)

So though I can know the wonders of heaven exist for me, assured by the Spirit, I do not know all this entails.

God has implanted in each of us the desire to live our earth life. This is the life we've known; it is the only one we have ever known; we are familiar with it, and in unnumbered ways we love it dearly. Relationships, though often difficult, have woven bonds of belongingness, security, and love, and we don't want to leave them. We are pulled between the desire for earthly life, and the longing for heaven and the life there. No one who is a believer and who is normal escapes this tug of war. Paul didn't (recall Philippians 1: 22–23). No one will. Why should I be surprised that I am not longing for death? I am not above being a person with normal feelings and desires, am I, no *matter* how strong my faith in heaven?

The actual experience of dying is another unknown. What will it be like? Will my faith prove valid? Is there truly life after death? No matter how great my belief, does not some doubt about this great unknown still linger? To the end it is a walk of faith, not proof. Some fear of the unknown is a certainty.

How then, I asked of God, can this fear be diminished? Can it be ended? As I asked this question, I sought the awareness of his presence with me. The promise is sure:

> . . . God has said,
> "Never will I leave you;
> never will I forsake you." (Hebrews 13:6)

The more I sought this awareness, the stronger it grew. I had walked and talked with this wonderful Lord for decades; I knew the reality of his presence with me daily. He was and has long been and is the great love of my life, my great God, my King, my best friend, my indwelling Lord. If I wasn't aware of his presence, it was because I chose not to be.

Here is the comfort of faith—God is here now! He will not leave. He will be present in all the days leading down to death, he will be present when I die, he will be present as I enter heaven, and he will be present with me in heaven. I will never experience this dying alone. I will have HIM. He knows my fear, but he himself, by his very person brings assurance that death is not the end. I have known HIM, and do know him, and can trust him with this day of my death.

But I trust in you, O Lord;

I say, "You are my God.

My times are in your hands" (Psalms 31:14-15a)

Do I trust him with my life? That is the question. I know I do, not just with belief but with the experience of his presence daily when I choose it. It is the joy of my heart, and therefore will be so every day of my old age and my journey down to death. I will walk it out with him, just as I have each day for many years, so that each day will follow another and the end will come when he is ready. He holds my hand. Sometimes I doubt and then miss the walk with him; I don't know why. I seem to flag or get lost in some project, Martha like, and just as distracted. Then I seek him again; he is there; he didn't leave.

With these thoughts and a release of my fear of death to him personally, my terror subsided. I did indeed leave and do leave to him the day of my death. Other questions arose for me, but this fear no longer tyrannized me. It arose again from time to time, but mainly because I felt there was unfinished business that needed to be attended to, and not because I feared my dying as I had previously. Even in regard to all the things I wanted to do, or thought I ought to do before I died, as I reviewed these with the Lord, I realized I could dismiss many of them as truly non-essential. Things I would need to do, he would enable me to do, one by one.

But now I know this: I am old—that's a fact—and I have a severe physical problem. I could die at any time. I have faced it, and I can truthfully say I am glad to have done so, for now the emotions have been included too, and I am no longer avoiding, rationalizing, nor denying the issue with all its attendant fears. With the continuing presence and assurance of Christ I do face the fear and find the peace in regard to my own death, whenever it comes.

Many fears beset the person who is experiencing diminishment. Whether the primary fear is fear of dying, or another just as terrifying or several others, each with its own tyranny, the first and foremost emotion one faces in diminshment is fear. What if's roar in: what if I lose my memory, what if my mind goes, what if I run out of money, what if no one wants to take care of me, what if I can no longer drive, what if I can't take care of myself? Beyond the personal are those questions about closest relationships: what if my husband dies first, what if my children put me in a home, what if I have to leave my friends and neighbors, what if . . . what if . . . what if?

As the fears arise, there is no escape from the accompanying feelings. With each I must enter in fully with the Lord—no hiding, no rationalizing, no minimizing. I pray that God will enable me to be fully transparent. He said the truth would set me free, so full truth must be faced. Then the ever important question is, "What is the Holy Spirit saying about this, here and now?" I believe Paul meant exactly what he said, "I am ready for anything through the strength of the one who lives within me." (Philippians 4:13, *The New Testament in Modern English*)

CHAPTER THREE

DIMINISHMENT

I think I have long believed that God still wants to heal today as he did in the days when Christ walked the earth. I believe we need to ask in faith for that gift of healing far more often and with more belief in his good will to do so, than we do. I also believe in all the gifts of medical knowledge he has given to enable that healing. I do know though that old people aren't always given the gift of healing, for it is in God's timing that he is bringing them down to their final days and giving the advance warning to prepare for home-going. I believe it is God's way of weaning them from earth and opening a growing desire for the joys of heaven.

I didn't, then, automatically assume that he would heal me; this might be my time for that "notice—time's up" from him to mark my final days. But frankly, it made me angry to think this. Why me? Why now? I am ministering for the kingdom! I addressed the Lord with my assumption, "Lord, I thought you valued the work I have been doing and would want it to continue! It makes no sense to cut it off now. Am I not valuable to you, to these ministries, to the people I serve? Surely you see this! So heal me, and I will testify to your greatness and healing power and love and give you great glory. Yes?" (Not exactly the end of pride, is it?)

I was incredibly frustrated during the days I waited in increasing weakness. Why did the Lord not open the doors for speedy medical treatment at least if that was the path of healing he was choosing for me? Why did I have to wait and know nothing in blind darkness? Was this fair?

Then the questions grew even greater. Why was there necessarily diminishment and debilitation in old age for most people? Why must there be such suffering? Why so much slowing and loss? It is humiliating to grow old, as all who are ageing know well from the never ceasing stream of jokes that flow from the e-mails, birthday greetings, and crass remarks of the young and not so young. It is bad enough to come to the end of life. Must there be all this additional loss of beauty, strength, stamina, and often brain power as well? I railed against it. "I don't like your plan, God; I thought you were kinder than that!"

As for me personally as I have stated previously, my illness meant a full STOP, not just a slowing down and finding time to smell roses. Why was this my lot?

After some time of this kind of pouring out my volatile emotions and toxic thinking, I remember asking the Lord for forgiveness, greatly needed, and then for revelation, and actually quieting myself to receive it. After a time, this is what I believe he gave me. One day I had a kind of awake dream; how can I explain? I was awake, but a sort of movie began in my mind. I was trudging down a road in a very dry, barren place with the Lord at my side. He was supporting me, for I was very tired and thirsty and near collapse. We came to some large rock formations on our right. They towered steeply about sixty feet high, some thirty wide. In one there was a small opening into the rock, and we turned to it and slipped through the opening. Inside I found, not a dark cave but a large room with a wide opening in the back into a spacious area of parkland. Rock surrounded the room like a large, round wall, and was totally open above to light and sky. Water seeped over the edge all along the left side, and on the ledges below grew hanging vines, green and lush, some filled with small flowers. I was reminded of the hanging gardens in Zion National Park. Though shadowed, it was beautiful and incredibly peaceful, and looked out on immense beauty.

The center contained a fully provisioned place to rest and be refreshed, with food and drink and comfortable bedding and cushions. It was obviously meant to be inhabited, a place of comfort and a place to rest down. I saw through the back opening a view of wonderful light with meadow and trees and loveliness, opening to a path that led through a beautiful garden filled with flowers of many colors and an arbor of roses. How bright and inviting it was, but I knew we weren't going there yet. I was certain in my heart, though, that the bright beauty of the garden path awaited me in the future.

Meanwhile I was to sit still with the Lord in the rock's interior dwelling. The Lord had brought me into this place of refuge for a reason he now clarified. He had me sit down and then, sitting beside me, he spread two huge wings around me, wings that held me immobile while at the same time gave me a sense of great safety and protection, of love and gentleness, and of great authority. He wordlessly instructed me to "Rest in" and I did so, leaning in and submitting to him. Peace washed over me.

Scriptures of these images flooded my mind:

From the ends of the earth I call to you,

I call to you as my heart grows faint;

lead me to the rock that is higher than I

For you have been my refuge,

a strong tower against the foe.

I long to dwell in your tent forever

and take refuge in the shelter of your wings. (Psalm 61:2–4)

My soul finds rest in God alone;

my salvation comes from him.

He alone is my rock and my salvation;

he is my fortress, I will never be shaken. (Psalm 62:1–2)

Because you are my help,

I sing in the shadow of your wings.

My soul clings to you;

Your right hand upholds me. (Psalm 63:7)

I sensed this envisioning was the Holy Spirit's way of applying these scriptures to me personally, so I asked him to tell me further why we were here and what it all meant.

Thoughts came that made it clear to me that a season of my life was ending and that I was to accept it. I would be learning a new season that would have a new mode of living; I needed to learn it; it was time; and the Lord could teach me only after I fully relinquished the old to him, with all its attendant habits and ways. This process would take some time of stillness and immobility. I would need to learn to "rest in" and trust him, far more than I ever had before. As I chose to do so, I would learn more and more of his marvelous nature and being, and that would be treasure greater than I had ever known. Would I be willing to suffer diminishment and debilitation to learn it? Oh yes, I thought, quite readily and firmly.

But as the days lingered while we sat in stillness, I knew this new learning would not be easy, for old habits drove me and pressured me and often shamed me for my inactivity. But he would not let go; I was held and would continue to be held in those loving wings and engaged in a severe mercy until I learned to rest and trust and then enter into that new mode of living. It did not come easily, and as I will tell, I often resisted mightily and still do from time to time, my head in one place, my heart in another.

I found beneath my loud clamor of how faithfully I had served him, I had another agenda—that I wanted to squeeze life of all it could offer before it ended, and that I was more than a little offended that this was not to be. It seemed unfair to me; I felt *entitled* to more. I had in years past already had to give up mountain hiking, biking, ice skating, and other such knee bending activities that I craved. I felt entitled to continue nature hikes and excursions, and of course a wide variety of social activities, dancing, and recreation, such as parasailing, kayaking, boating, and riding gondolas up mountain peaks. I wanted to keep on traveling too, and adventuring in the discovery of new places and people and cultures. I wanted to try new things as well and to have the energy to do them. I wanted to learn new skills on the computer, and to operate all the wonderful new electronic wizardry coming on the market, along with the vocabulary that went with it, all of which required a stamina and endurance I no longer had. I didn't want my teenage grandkids ceasing to tell me I was a fun grandmother who would still ride Disneyland rides, plunge into pools, play competitive games with them, take them on outings and in general prove to them I was still the life of the party.

All of these activities ended for me at that time. I had no stamina to begin new ones. Not fair, I complained; no, not fair at all. The Lord challenged me; why did I think I was entitled to continue these activities? Entitled, that's the word, for I strongly felt that I was due them. Why? I had no answer. Other questions erupted. Was I trying to prove myself younger than I was? Was I trying to impress not only my grandchildren but the rest of the world too? Most importantly, what was I trying to do to myself; was I refusing to grow old? Why did I make efforts to do these strenuous things? Weren't there also enjoyments for an old person? What else could I learn to do? Weren't there intriguing things to be learned that I had never tried, even in a weakened state?

Yet I reasoned that all these former activities I sought to continue were good for me, wholesome and beneficial, so why couldn't I keep having them? Again I believe the Lord was telling me that this season of my life had *ended*, and that I was to learn that new dimension he would teach me. But I closed my ears to this inner hearing. Since I could not know it in advance, since I could not control it, I didn't think it could possibly be as good or better than what I knew. How could it be?

But what choice did I have? I could be resentful of curtailment and diminishment, or I could accept it and join him wholeheartedly in new adventure on a new level. I had said yes to him too quickly before consideration. Now I had lengthy, intense, resistant second thoughts, and I admit I alternated for a long while between the two choices, and as I did so, the Lord held me immobile under his wings. Perhaps if I resisted the changes and had faith that I would be healed, then it would likely be only a matter of patient waiting. Perhaps I needed more faith, more claiming the victory. I turned to the Lord, who held me immobile, and began to listen. For the most part, silence reigned, but I strongly sensed the Lord's calm and reserve in it, and his strong resolve to hold me to his will.

It became clearer: I had a choice, not to go back as I insisted, but either to become resentful and embittered, or to accept his will for me in this new season.

It might be difficult to change habits, but I needed to trust God that he wanted the very best for me, and was offering it if I would only trust him. It opened to the bright land of joy that lay beyond the rock enclosure. What new things were there? What would I now learn and do as I never yet had?

We who enter old age with true acceptance experience a change of seasons and life style, whether abruptly or slowly, that is truly different and of an unknown quality until we embrace it. Many of our experiences will not be new or different from what we have known, but will be of a different nature in the way we experience them. Forced to slowness we will receive them with a depth and understanding that we previously lacked.

If I regain the strength I once had, I will resume the activities I enjoy. But if not, and at present this is the case, I will continue to invite and receive the new experiences in store for me from a loving, giving God. I find this means I walk a slower pace, but I have gradually come to see more, sense more, be fully aware of more, and to take it in more deeply. Colors shine and blend; I see a leaf; I am captured by the color and fragrance of a flower. Bird songs pour into my ear. I eat slowly, tasting my food and relishing it. And somehow in a way I find very hard to express, all these sensory experiences which I once reached out for so passionately now *come* to me with a heightened and deepened awareness and comprehension I find remarkable. I sense the Lord's presence deeply as I experience these gifts from him and with him. He is delighted with my enjoyment of these things and my increasing gratitude for them. And people—but more about that later.

As we ageing ones accept with trust this new dimension, we also find it an interior land of exploration, of expansion, that our former daily lives had not known. This came to me not only in expansion of my senses, it came to me in the music I heard, in the books I selected, in the programs I watched, in the walks I took, and in the relationships I treasured. Having time now to linger and to contemplate, I entered in deeply, realizing the experiences of my own responses and sharing those in dialog with the Lord. I also more acutely entered into the experiences and responses of those I read about, savoring their thoughts and mine as well. I found I had no sense of pressure to get on with it, to finish, to hurry through. I could now allow for genuine meditation.

I was beginning to trust God in regard to his plan, to let go of the former ways, and to dare to learn what he was eager and joyful to show me. I had more letting go to do, but in time I would do so, and turn to the new. The process had begun and continues. This was the beginning of glad adventures on the last mile home.

CHAPTER FOUR.

WHOSE BODY?

For decades I have held the belief that my body is, as Scripture teaches, the temple, the dwelling place of God, his possession: "Do you not know that your body is a temple of the Holy Spirit, who is in you, whom you have received from God? You are not your own; you were bought at a price. Therefore honor God with your body." (1 Corinthians 6: 19–20)

I have long thought that I had given my body wholly to the Lord, and was now a steward of it for his sake. Considering its care a sacred trust, I was careful to maintain the best health I possibly could. I ate a healthful diet that I believed honored the Lord—"He who eats meat, eats to the Lord, for he gives thanks to God; and he who abstains, does so to the Lord and gives thanks to God" (Romans 14:6) I exercised consistently on a daily basis whenever possible and was careful to get a good night's sleep. Seeking to keep my weight within healthful boundaries (not thin, mind you, but medium, at most), I fought valiantly, in my opinion, reducing fats and sweets, when I went over my limit by a few pounds. Yearly health check-ups were never omitted. If you detect a note of pride in this list, you are right, I'm sure, though I thought my motives were honorable. I could say truthfully that I took the best care I could of my body because it was for the Lord's use.

How surprised I was when my body began to fail! How could it fail me like this? At first I thought, of course, that my condition was temporary. But as it worsened and lengthened, I had to conclude, with fear and anger and great sorrow, that this might be permanent! I could hardly believe it.

Then it dawned on me that if my body was truly the Lord's possession and not mine, that he could do with it whatever he chose. But I was shocked that he chose, after all my good care of it, to render it almost useless. I realized I had assumed (another assumption!) that he would want to keep it healthy and active and fully functioning until the end, so that I could use it for his service in a maximum way.

Then I came to realize my own true motivation which had been hidden to me: I had been keeping fit for my own pleasure primarily. That revelation surprised me tremendously. When healthy, I was able to do an amazing array of the things I most enjoyed as I have previously described. When any one of them was suggested, or I had the impulse to go and do, I just did it without a moment's hesitation. It seemed to me that I should avail myself of the pleasure. I didn't engage in prayer and consultation with the Lord at those times; I just went with pure conviction that it was my due. The Lord would want me to have fun, wouldn't he? I'd be off and running before I had waited for an answer to that. I didn't ask it actually. I just assumed that having fun was a side benefit of pleasing God, an assumption I acted on without thought.

Now I saw that I had deceived myself. I hadn't truly relinquished my body to him fully; much of its use I had kept for myself.

More frequent was my sense of my appearance—surely this was my choice, wasn't it? I wanted particularly to retain as much beauty as possible and still do. I don't think I can overstate how strong this desire is. And I do believe it is not just a personal issue with me; I think the vast majority of women are consumed by the longing to be and to remain as beautiful as they can possibly be for as long as possible. Look at the array of commercials on TV; note the multitudinous super slick magazines ads. Every other one is about a female retaining her beauty—with diet, exercise, skin care, cosmetics, eye beauty, hair color and style, removal of wrinkles, manicures and pedicures, and myriad aspects of all of these. What have I forgotten? My thinking: this is MY body to keep as attractive as I can for as long as I can.

Age has very little to do with it. I find this vanity aspect in older women as well as pre-teens and every age in between. Why? What is the motive? Surely it is to see the admiration in another's eyes (and my own). If I receive it, I know I qualify, I know I have value. I am valuable if others deem I look good; if not, I'm not. And why is that so important? Simply put, it is the core of a woman's self-esteem. Perhaps it is that ever present longing in each girl to snag the good-looking guy—and to be envied for doing so. It's that, but far more, because it doesn't end with marriage. This desire for beauty is life-long, to the last minute of clear mindedness. Whether it's innate or the influence of our culture, I couldn't say (let the experts debate), but I simply know it is there, snagging me with every glance in the mirror. Truth—I don't just want others to admire my looks; I want to be at the top, more attractive than any other. It's an ego thing.

I certainly do not advocate an unkempt appearance, slothfulness, or indifference to body care; these show a disregard for the body as the temple of God. And I do believe he would have us look as good as we can for as long as we can, holding valuable what he has given us. But that's a far cry from the compulsive, all absorbing attention we women give to our appearance and the comments we hope to solicit. Where is the true will of God in this matter of the body?

The never-ending jokes about the way women love shopping contain a large measure of truth. Do we really need all this attention to clothing, fashion, the latest fad, the most updated apparel? Why must my body be draped in new clothing? Why is the old not good enough? Is this the will of God while women in the third world countries pull on the same dreary dress day after day? What about shoes? How many pairs are enough? Purses? Doesn't God want us to enjoy these things, I reason. I know he knows we love new things; we give him thanks for them, surely. Am I supposed to feel guilty every time I buy myself a new skirt, a new pair of shoes, a new handbag?

Now I mulled these questions as I was challenged afresh by Romans 12:1: "Therefore, I urge you, brothers, in view of God's mercy, to offer your bodies as living sacrifices, holy and pleasing to God—this is you spiritual act of worship." Was I truly willing that my body belong fully and completely to him to do with just as he pleased, or did I want to maintain control for my own purposes? The question was searching. "In view of God's mercy"—how merciful God had been to me to give me life, health, and vigor for so many years! How gracious he had been to me to give me salvation, love, kindness, care and attention. How full of mercy. How truly undeserving I was of all he had done in and through my life.

Could I yield my body truly to him? Could my motive be pure in doing so? Would I keep pleading for healing and restoration, for retaining beauty and youthfulness, for affording all that would keep me looking fashionable and fetching, or would I give over the choice to him completely, knowing my body was his to use or not use as he chose?

Did I now truly have a choice? Perhaps he would choose death for me; I could not oppose it. He had chosen debilitation for me; I could not oppose it. Perhaps he would choose to heal me fully; I could not control it. Perhaps he would choose to have me relinquish all vanity and the quest to stay beautiful. I could not change his choice.

But I could choose a glad giving over of my body to him, whatever he chose to do. I could choose to consider his will in every choice I made regarding it. I could begin to hear his will truly in regard to this temple I called his. I could choose.

Or I could choose to keep trying to get him to do my will, and restore my body to my use and pleasure. If I chose to insist on health, and he did not give it, how would I react? If I chose spending time and money on my appearance as I pleased, and still found myself growing more unattractive—wrinkled, gray, dim-eyed, sagging, over weight, stooped—how would I feel towards him? Could I be wholehearted in my willingness to forego owning my body? Yet this is exactly what Romans 12:1 instructed me to do. I was to give over *ownership and control* to him.

I knew I could not do this giving over without the full enablement of the Holy Spirit. The loss was too great and I was grieving it greatly. But the choice was mine, and frankly I was not at ease with it. I did not want death, or debilitation, or diminishment with increasing unattractiveness. I did not want chronic illness, or wasting energy, or old ladies' clothing and appearance. I wanted the maximum health and beauty and vitality, and then, when I was ninety, a gentle slide into reduced mobility and activity and pace of living, or just a quick ending to it all. That was long years away. I knew clearly what *I* wanted.

But he is worthy! Worthy of all I am and have. This was abundantly clear to me in view of God's mercies. If I was to know him fully and trust him completely, I had to choose to give my body and all that concerned it to him as "my spiritual service." I stewed awhile over the whole issue, and did not hide my true feelings from him. Quite a few of my journal entries are either bemoaning the unfairness of my weak estate, or bargaining with him for a way back to health and good appearance, or making an effort to control the outcome of my medical treatment.

Facing up to what was happening to me was remarkably hard and still is. One of the most alarming things that befell me from the medications prescribed, particularly prednisone, was a sudden and continuing weight gain (then over 30 pounds and climbing later to over 60). Yes, I now had more energy, and could go places, but now I hardly wanted to, with this new ugliness. I was horrified, helpless to curtail it, and very depressed by it. I couldn't bear getting on the scales, yet I couldn't keep myself from doing so. I had to know. Oh, bad news again. Another pound. And another. I no longer fit into my clothes. I lumbered along, off balance, and looked peculiar to myself in what I did wear.

I was also seeing the effects in my face. It became full, my eyes slanted, my cheeks rounded. And now I sprouted whiskers, side-burns, and heavy dark eye brows. I was not me! Who was this? Far from getting used to my new appearance, I was repelled by it! One look and I felt shame and guilt as if I were truly responsible by sloth, indulgence, and indifference for the changes. I knew I was not, but once again head and heart did not agree.

Perhaps the worst part was what I saw in the eyes of others— astonishment and embarrassed discomfort. I sensed their struggle to say something. "How good to see you! You are looking good!" When I heard these words, I knew they meant it. They were glad to see me as well as I was, glad I was up, about, moving. But they couldn't mask their surprise when they first saw me after many weeks and sometimes months at how changed I was. One or two blurted the truth, "I'd never have known you."

Perhaps this issue doesn't seem different from that I presented in the previous chapter. For me, they were two separate though related issues. The first issue was resting in God's choice to remove the *activities* I enjoyed. This issue was surrendering my *body* and all that concerned it to him for his choices.

The battle raged for months. Full surrender was what I needed to give. Finally, I did. What would this now mean? I didn't know. I wrote this verse in my journal: "Therefore, I urge you, brothers, in view of God's mercy, to offer your bodies as living sacrifices, holy and pleasing to God—this is your spiritual act of worship." (Romans 12:1)

I continued with these thoughts:

"If I see you, Jesus, worship you rather than seek a quick fix, then as my act of worship, nothing is truly even reasonable except to give you *all* I have: my whole self, my *body*.

Here, Lord, I hand you this body, this me.

It is not holy except you make it holy . . . I must give it totally and completely into your hands. What will you do with it?

Other scripture phrases come to mind: ' . . . the Author and Finisher of our faith' and also, " . . . run with patience the race that is set before you.'"

I did know that if he restored my health to the previous level, I would no longer be able to assume I could use my body as I chose. I would need to be careful to seek his will in its use and appearance, even for those pleasurable things I had once considered my right.

My day would have to be walked out under his direction regardless of what I wanted. Full new ownership meant consulting him on each issue. I did now know I was fully dependent on the Lord himself to keep me to this choice. I prayed not to deceive myself again. This was a new position for me in this new season of my life. I still find myself following after old habits, thinking negative thoughts, and so having to reject them immediately. I find myself having to turn again and again to him to yield my body to him afresh. "This body belongs to you, Lord. Do with it as you will." I find myself needing to say that to him many times each day. I expect I will continue this learning daily on the last mile home to the finish.

CHAPTER FIVE

GLORY GIRL

I confess readily that my foremost besetting sin has always been pride. I remember that as I child I was always pretending to be a performer, a song and dance girl or a Hollywood star, that dazzled people with my performance and inspired them to praise me extravagantly. I think I never lost that motivation to hear the adulation, the word of admiration, the applause. "Isn't she just fabulous!" "There is just no one like her!" "What awesome teaching!" All music to me. Not that these comments were said in my presence except now and then, but I imagined them being said often by those who heard my teaching or who came to me for counseling, and it gave me great pleasure to hear it in my mind. I reveled in the glory though I denied it and hid it from my own knowledge as well as I could.

Yet I hated my pride and the longings it brought. I knew, and I know, that all that I am, any talents I have, the temperament I have, the aptitudes I have developed—all were given to me by God. Paul questioned the haughty Corinthians: "For who makes you different from anyone else? What do you have that you did not receive? And if you did receive it, why do you boast as though you did not?" (1 Corinthians 4:7) I think we really do not believe that. Yet when I reflect on what I myself have produced alone, on what I have done with my will power, on what I can call my own, then I realize that every action I name is NOT my own. None could exist without God's provision.

It is obvious rationally that we did not furnish ourselves with these bodies of ours, not a bit of it, and that of course, includes the brain. I have merely chosen to preserve and use (or neglect and abuse) what I have been given. And I have long known well that unless the Holy Spirit is empowering the performance in me, and I am giving glory to God through it, it is all "wood, hay, or straw." (1 Corinthians 3:12) Knowing didn't take away my secret longings though, and these I have had to face over and over, as they have crept back into their hiding places after being evicted.

Realizing that much of my serving God, down through the years, whether behind the scenes or up front, had been done with mixed motives brought me great shame. Oh I did want to be God's instrument through which he poured himself out to others. But . . . underneath lay the hidden motive: I longed to gain glory for me. How it stung to realize that! But that was the truth that I had to face with God.

I recalled the origins of my life-long habit of gaining glory by performance. When I was about five I discovered my true calling: I was slated to be a song and dance girl. This discovery came early; it was formed from going to movies with my older brother on Saturday afternoons. The matinees of that era featured two movies, a cartoon, and a fifteen minute serial to entertain all the children in the audience. Parents parked their children there for about three hours while they shopped and visited and enjoyed the day. What a rowdy bunch we were. The teenage ushers armed with flashlights had a great time strutting their stuff and using their power to bark corrections and to oust the incorrigible.

My favorite part of the afternoon was the western which always featured a saloon segment. The dance hall girls would come on stage and do their saucy routine, kicking high and twirling and sashaying around, drawing hoots and hollers and whistles from the multitude of cowboys watching them. How I dreamed of being one of them! I loved to dress up and I loved to dance, so that was a wonderful combination. Most of all I loved to get the notice and approval that such a performance would bring. Ah the sheer joy of getting those sounds of admiration sparked my imagination to the maximum.

"Roll out the barrel. We'll have a barrel of fun . . . " Picture this five year old on the front porch as I belted out my song while flinging my legs and feet in a woeful parody of the dance hall queen's routine. If Daddy had a night time job and was trying to sleep, Momma would come hurrying out to shush me, and send me off to quieter pursuits. Off I would go to the far corners of the property, still rehearsing in my imagination my marvelous routine and all the sounds of praise and admiration pouring forth for *me*! Ambition grew as fantasy abounded.

In the years that followed, my fantasies of glory changed, but not my desire to have it. I often "played to the gallery," longing for those sounds of approval, applause, and praise. Soul candy. Sweet music. Addictive.

In my university years, I trained to be a teacher. I was from a teaching family— my maternal grandfather, grandmother, and aunt were public school teachers. My mother also had the teaching urge—she taught Sunday school for twenty-five years. The genes were there; it was my DNA. I fantasized being a teacher in my child play, but this fantasy truly was a possibility. When I did become a teacher, I also became a performer. I loved to give my teaching a dramatic aspect and act it out with panache, for I loved the performance and the praise that followed. "Song and dance girl."

Later, when I began to teach Bible studies, I followed the same procedures in my presentations. I relished the comments that followed, and planned each lesson so that I could glean them. Then the Lord began to make a close examination of my heart and to show me that I was robbing him of glory, depending on my flesh, and not allowing the power of the Holy Spirit to come through. My pride took a real nose-dive. It took me years to quickly discern when I practiced a take-over and exerted my performance mode. By the time of my fall in the creek, I was still needing this discernment. My pride constantly sought resurrection and manifested itself in my performance mode now and then. Oh to get before a crowd and to solicit laughs and responses! Still candy to my soul. But utter poison.

With my fall and my nephritis and the full stop, I now had no opportunity for performance or glory.

For my seventy-fifth birthday, my husband George had wanted to give me a big party, and allow all my friends to give me lots of love and gratitude and praise. I said no because I knew I would not only expect much adulation, but bask in it when I got it. The temptation was too strong. Secretly I hoped some friend might give me a surprise party so I would not have to say no, and could relish the glory while acting surprised. Is your heart as thoroughly deceitful as mine? I would come away from such thoughts just hating and despairing of myself. As the old song so aptly puts it, " . . . and pour contempt on all my pride." Then I would turn to the Lord in my shame and confess this sin of pride again. How humiliating! I would pour out my sin and my self-loathing to him, declare my utter helplessness to overcome, throw myself on his mercy, and finally, exhausted, stop castigating myself. I would then ask him to enable me to receive his forgiveness, rest in his love once again, and bring glory to *Him*.

But there would be no party for my seventy-fifth birthday, not given by George or any one else. I was too weak to celebrate. By September I put away all thought of it, large or small. George did as I asked him and arranged a short and happy lunch on my birthday with Greg and Colleen, two of our best friends, and we called it a day. It was all I could manage.

I grieved some more now and then about lost opportunities for performance, and then confessed again as solid sin all my desire for glory and acclaim of any kind. There would be no more, even if I sought it. I was out, pure and simple—laid low, shelved, eliminated. That would solve my pride problem. Perhaps the Lord had had enough of my repeated glory-seeking, and so he had seen to it that there would be no more.

Now a related problem arose. I realized I was now nothing in the performance department, a nobody, and sick at that. Because I could do no works I felt that I had no value to anyone. I felt negated and wondered who I was now (more about this identity crisis in the following chapter), lamenting that all my ministries were at an end. Even though for years I had prayed and sought to perform *in* the Spirit and *to* the glory of God, I loved the work he had assigned me to do, but now it was over. I grieved this immensely. Not only could I not perform, I couldn't serve in any way.

After a time I realized the Lord was telling me something insistently. These verses began to fill my mind:

"For we are God's workmanship, created in Christ Jesus to do good works, which God prepared in advance for us to do." (Ephesians 2:10)

"God is not unjust; he will not forget your work and the love you have shown him as you have helped his people and continue to help them." (Hebrews 6:10)

"And his master replied, 'Well done, good and faithful servant! . . . *Come and share your master's happiness.*'" (Matthew 25:23, emphasis mine)

Those last words reminded me of the King James Version: *"Enter into the joy of your Master."* I heard them again and again in my mind. That's when I realized that the Lord was telling me that he not only appreciated all I had done down through the years—all that *was* done in his Spirit—but that he was celebrating it now, right now, and asking me to join him, asking me to receive his thankfulness for me. He was giving me his own party. I was to "enter into the joy" he himself was feeling.

I asked that he might make known to me what was meant by "the joy of your Master." What was his joy in this? When I examined the parable he told (Matthew 25:14–30), I saw that he rejoiced in seeing that what he had provided—money—had been taken and utilized and made productive, and the increase brought back to him. It gave him great satisfaction to celebrate his good stewards. Regarding the works I had done, the time given, the ministries performed, even with mixed motives on my part, the gold that was there remained, and he rejoiced to see it and celebrate it with me. He valued it with joy.

I still had to grieve my lost abilities, yet I did manage to receive thankfully the joy he had in me, and that was very comforting to me. Now I realized that there might never be another restoration to service, but if not, I needed to remember his joy in what had been, and not to forget that he treasured it. My audience of One provided all the applause I needed.

It took awhile for me to be able to accept his joy, and to joy with him. It stole over me like a slow smile.

Yet I knew that if ministry was restored or new ministry given, I would still be tempted to gain glory for myself by my performance. Now having increased awareness, I prayed to remember what he had taught me.

By spring of 2008 I felt well enough to teach a short course on the Lord's Prayer. Sensing the Lord asking me to do this and praying that he guard my heart from seeking any acclaim, I relied on him for content, presentation, and delivery. When teaching time arrived, I had never felt so free and free-flowing in the power of the Spirit. There was no problem with glory-seeking this time. Instead I experienced a great joy and a sense of privilege to be proclaiming his words and teaching, and no temptation to judge myself, measure responses, or seek compliments. My experience was "from him, through him, to him" (Romans 11:36). His gladness filled me.

I could now go on to discover with him whatever new realms of living he had in mind for me, no matter what they were, on the last mile home. I couldn't guess what they might be, diminished as I was, but when he wanted further service, he would supply me energy for it, and he would open the doors to it. Now my problem was different. I must await his will and timing, and not *try* to find a ministry. My love of involvement and action had yet to be tempered. But learn I would, though I chomped at the bit now and then. He didn't budge. I needed to learn that I would not go out on any commission until my Master was ready to send me. That call was entirely his. Until then, my call was to enter in to the joy of my Master.

CHAPTER SIX

WHO AM I?

At least thirty years ago, the big emphasis on self-esteem was in full swing. I also remember how women at that time were intrigued by learning their "colors"—which hues and shades they should select for clothes and make-up that would most enhance their natural skin and hair coloring. We all asked for help in getting color typed. I have always loved fall colors, but found out that they did not suit me for clothes. The colors most complimentary to me were called "winter." I didn't feel like winter, but I could see I looked better in forest green than in fall gold. I did like it that "winter" included those hues called jewel tones.

Then I thought of all this revelation about colors as an analogy to a woman's inner being. What were our inner colors? What were mine? It was very clear to me that each of us had been given our inner colors by our Maker. I prepared an address to women called "God's Design." I asked each woman to let God define her, and to let God enable her to know and live out her own inner colors. I compared each woman's inner being to a prism of crystal. As God's light shone through the prism, it gave off beautiful, unique, and extraordinary rays of color. Of course, prisms give off the same colors; we give off those put in us by God when we allow His light to shine through. And the glowing colors are unique to each individual.

Another analogy I used was that of stained glass windows. A master artist such as Chagall designs a beautiful stained glass window, a work of art that shines in all its glory and beauty only when the light behind it is full and radiant and penetrating. God is the Light; each of us is a window which he wants to light up and to set aglow the colors he has put there. Conclusion: my true identity is his design; it shines forth in my being and in my doing when I am allowing his light to shine through. I am who HE says I am; he does through me what he will, and when filled with light it is beautiful, for he has made it so.

In another way of looking at this God design, the Bible says each of us is a vessel designed for his use (See Romans 9:23, 2 Corinthians 4:7, and 2 Timothy 2:20–21). So it is never *being* versus *doing*. It is always both/and. I am, therefore I do. My being does precede my doing and yet my doing does not define my identity. His workmanship alone defines me and gives me my identity. I do not need to worry about what vessel I am nor what he is doing with it. He will use it as he will, when he will, where he will. I need to trust that I am his design and he will fulfill the purpose for which he created me.

Now I wish I had remembered all that when, as I mentioned before, along with the ceasing of all ministry there came an overwhelming sense of being lost. By this I mean I questioned my identity. The question kept popping up in me, "Who am I now?" It puzzled me. I was still myself, wasn't I? And yet I did not know myself in this weakened state. This just wasn't the Joy I knew: that person was active and vigorous and always on the go. How could I be me, just lying there in stagnation, staring out the window, watching the world go by? How did I define myself now?

Had my personality changed? My intellect? My habits? My attitudes, interests, curiosity? How much of the *inner* me was changed by this debilitation? The great reduction in energy made me doubt myself on every question.

Yes, all had changed; all was weakened and ineffectual. I was not that active person any longer. I was an old woman and I didn't want to be. I didn't want to be this person I'd become. I didn't like this person. She was filled with sadness; she was weepy, whiney, and given to self-pity, always lamenting something or other. Tiresome and boring, she couldn't seem to muster much interest in anything. I hated being in her body. I didn't know her and didn't want to. I felt like two people, the former imprisoned by the latter, my whole condition confusing me greatly. But I was at least facing the truth head-on. Or so I thought.

My plea burst from me again and again, "God restore me! Give me back myself, and I will praise you all my days." But the self I knew wasn't being restored. The changed self remained. A weak, elderly person was now the real person, the "I am." How could this be a good thing God had handed me? How could Scripture say, "And we know that in all things—*all things*—God works for the good of those who love him, who have been called according to his purpose"? (Romans 8:28, emphasis mine) Wasn't I in that category? If all things were working together for my good, I could in no way see it. Over and over, my question, "How can this change be for good?"

I would set my mind to believe God's truth, but I couldn't stay with it. The question arose again and again.

My major problem became clear: I indeed *did* equate my identity with my doing. In my journal I wrote on Oct 24, 2007:

All this stripping away of pride, possession, patterns—it is for no future. There is no goal or vision, no hope. Why is it so very important that I be useful again? All I can see now is how *useless* I am. I see the world, its billions and I am nothing within it. Why is it so very important to you, God, that I be made *nothing*? If you are taking me home, why this process now? Is this a weaning away, or is it a refiner's fire? I only know that now, in my present state, I am useless to you—and that uselessness is very distressing, depressing, even devastating.

I am in a very dark place, and it is night. I cannot see in any direction, even behind. I only know one thing; I am under your wing in a place called *refuge* and we seem not to be moving. I must learn to *be* here. At present I haven't. I am yearning to hurry up and learn and get out of here!

In pondering the concept of *being* before God, "I confess my realization that I am afraid of intimacy—of just being with a person, of being seen and known for who I am, not for my knowing or having answers or dispensing wisdom. No wonder I try to end it, to get away. Yet God knows me intimately and entirely. I am afraid of him—of what he will show me of myself."

"Do I like me? Have I ever? I don't think I do. I like my doings (or did) but I think I don't like who I am. Why would I? I am so sinful, devious, and disdainful. Does Jesus just love the Holy Spirit in me or does he love *me* too? I will only know the answer to this as I stay in his presence."

Then one morning, before dawn, I awakened with this thought: "John Milton was right; 'they also serve who only stand and wait.'"

The plea of the Apostle Paul came to mind. You remember his condition:

> To keep me from becoming conceited because of these
> surpassingly great revelations, there was given me a thorn in my
> flesh, a messenger of Satan, to torment me. Three times I pleaded
> with the Lord to take it away from me. But he said to me, "My

grace is sufficient for you, for my power is made perfect in weakness." Therefore I will boast all the more gladly about my weaknesses, so that Christ's power may rest on me . . . For when I am weak, then I am strong. (2 Corinthians 12:7–10)

What did that mean to me? These thoughts then flooded my mind: I belong to the Lord to define, not to myself, not to my actions, not to my works or ministry. I belong to God. First, he is my Creator, he formed me in my mother's womb and I indeed am "fearfully and wonderfully made, your works are wonderful, I know that full well" (Psalm 139: 14). He provided my God design—my inner colors—and that does not change. I will be that person until death, regardless of strength or weakness. Energy is not the issue. Stamina is not the issue. Health is not the issue. My being remains. That identity is not lost to God.

But he also redeemed me for his own use: "For we are God's workmanship, created in Christ Jesus to do good works, which God prepared in advance for us to do." (Ephesians 2:10) He knows what he wants me to *do*. I am his to instruct every day. He may change his plan and program for me at any time—that is his prerogative as Master. He may add or reduce. He may set me aside or expend me fully. I am to trust his choosing for me. In his parables, the Master assigns the funds and gives the instructions. Do I maintain fellowship with him while I stand and wait? Do I enjoy and adore him when he gives no assignment? No amount of waiting changes my identity or my value!

I have another fear. It is the temptation to fail to hear him. I am afraid I will come to like the irresponsibility of diminishment. By that I mean I find myself thinking, "All right, I have no energy to do much. So I won't. I'll just laze around and do whatever I want to." I will not hear what I *am* able to do with the energy he gives. I will miss the new assignment, the glad engagement in the challenge that exists on a small scale but which has true significance. This temptation is great; lethargy is strong; the enemy's lies are constant. The Lord gives me a strong way of escape out of this temptation—it is summarized in his two words, "Follow me." I must keep my eyes on him and watch. What I see him do in my spirit, I must do. It will not be too much for me, and I must claim no exemptions. No rationalizations will do, no distractions prevail.

He is right now still engaged in the process of sanctifying me. He is today, even in my elder years, continuing to conform me to the image of Jesus Christ in my character. My core identity formed by God does not change, yet I will be changing in my inner being and my outer behavior until the day I die, as I am willing. This process doesn't end.

So I conclude that God defines me everyday. I am both being and becoming. I walk it out with him every mile of the way, including the last one. Life with God is adventure or nothing. My focus on myself ceases. My focus on him needs to stay constant, for he defines all. I can trust him still.

These thoughts eased my troubled mind and blessed me with their truth.

A new question arose: What am I like when I am experiencing this union? I could in no way find an answer to this, for union with him is just that—union. I am not concerned then about who I am; I am filled with the incredible sense of oneness with Jesus. How truly amazing that is. Self-identity is no longer a consideration. How could it be?

But don't I have a personal soul to consider? Where do soul and spirit divide? These questions led me to my next quest of discovery on this journey.

CHAPTER SEVEN

OH MY SOUL

Much emphasis is placed on the body today. But this is also the era of the soul. Everything must be performed with *soul* (or *heart*, meaning the same thing as soul when used this way). All must see that the skater skates with soul, not just artistry; that the dancer spins with soul, not just technique; that the runner gives it his all, not just his speed; that the President or Prime Minister speaks with soul (from the heart), not just with intellect.

Not that the concept of soul is clearly defined; it isn't. It is *felt*. All can feel it when it is there, can we not?

But how does one define this elusive word, soul?

Down through the years I have had many questions and many impressions, but no clear explanation of just what the soul is. In our unabridged dictionary, *The Random House Dictionary of the English Language, Second Edition*, I read the following as the first definition:

"The principle of life, feeling, thought in human beings, . . . the spiritual part of human being as distinct from the physical part."[1] Clear? Not to me. Soul: part of my God design, my identity, yes. But nevertheless, subject to development, change, growth, distortion. Emotional—yes. Passionate—yes. Source or home of my thought life—yes. Is it my brain?

Scripture tells me that I am a three part being. 1 Thessalonians 5:23: "May your whole spirit, soul and body be kept blameless at the coming of our Lord Jesus Christ." Hebrews 4:12-13 declares: "For the word of God is living and active. Sharper than any double-edged sword, it penetrates even to dividing soul and spirit, joints and marrow; it judges the thoughts and attitudes of the heart."

Ephesians 2:1 declares: "As for you, you were dead in your transgressions and sins . . . " I have been taught that this "dead" means spirit. Jesus said, "Flesh gives birth to flesh, but the Spirit gives birth to spirit." (John 3:6) That seems very clear to me.

It would seem then that the unbeliever accepts the definition of soul as containing man's spirit, and that a very alive part of him. He certainly does not see himself as dead in spirit, though the Bible says he is. Yet *spirit*, that part made to be brought to life and filled by God, is certainly dead; that is, unconnected, unborn in relation to the God Who created it. But alive in *soul?* Yes, indeed! The unbeliever sees body and soul as constituting the sum total of his person. How much "soul" he has is a large measure of his worth and value. He develops many "soul loves" and "soul pursuits." He puts "soul" into as much as he can, and draws on soul to give meaning and fullness to his experiences. Soul delights him. Believers may not agree that the spirit is part of the soul, but they too believe in the soul, relish it, engage it, enjoy it, celebrate it, pray with it, and give thanks to God for it, even if it cannot be exactly defined. It is certainly so for me.

During this time of change in my life I realized that much in life that had given me delight was now missing. My "soul loves" had once meant the essence of living to me. Loving great art and the contemplation of it, I sought it out or meditated on it, haunting art galleries. The same was true of music. I could lose myself in a great symphony or concerto, or even a romantic love song, and I had relished the wonderful nuances of melody and harmony as I experienced them. I had fed my soul longing on fine music. Or standing before a masterpiece of nature, enthralled by the beauty and wonder of it all, I would find my heart overflowing with gratitude to the Creator for it. I had thirsted for such experiences, and had travelled hundreds of miles to have them.

I recalled gazing in wonder at the Sistine Chapel, at Michelangelo's David, at the Mona Lisa, at Rafael's masterpieces. Each drew me in to the heart of the art, creating questions about the person portrayed; each somehow rendered me part of the subject, filled with an empathy for the moment of experience I was viewing.

I recalled concerts featuring Chopin or Mozart or Beethoven. The music likewise wrapped me in its torrents of sound and emotion, creating whole interior landscapes and experiences in me. How joyously I joined in the singing of great hymns of the church—I well remember mornings in chapel in Wheaton College, joining with 1700 other exuberant voices, singing "Wonderful Grace of Jesus." Glorious!

I recalled my rapture at viewing Yosemite Falls where my tears of awe and joy burst forth at the magnificence. The Grand Canyon had rendered me awestruck, statue still in wonder and disbelief. How often had sunsets, sunrises, ocean views, massive waterfalls created those peak moments of awareness of the grandeur of God as seen in his creation.

Also the mind: I had delighted in learning new things; I had delighted in being intelligent and perceptive and wise (or so I thought).

What pleasure it had brought to my soul to read books, to see quality movies and TV, to feast on good teaching and profound sermons.

How beautiful, receptive, and glorious is the soul of man! How I have loved engaging my soul. I am grateful for every such experience I have had. How good God has been in giving me so many and so much richness of soul experience and learning. Yet there was a snare in it all. Having soul experiences became a kind of addiction. For years I sought, craved, and fed ravenously on my soul experiences and didn't feel alive unless I had them. I lived from thrill to thrill, constantly reaching for more.

When I gave my life fully to Christ, I slowly came to learn how woven are our soul longings with our sinful nature. How greatly we desire to use all the powers and provisions of the soul to demonstrate our superiority, to forge ahead, to have power, to amass riches, to be the best so that we can worship ourselves and reveal our godhood. When we reach to get, to grasp, to have, to obtain, we indeed may gain the whole world, yes, but somehow lose our souls in the process. This puzzles and confuses the natural man when we Christians point this out, because for him, as I have said, gaining the master proficiency of soul and body is the true game of life. Those who do are the winners; those who don't are losers.

As I grew in my Christian faith, I came to realize that I was now to be ruled by the Holy Spirit and that HE would orchestrate the use of my soul. He, the Holy Spirit, through my spirit, would direct and lead and employ every facet of my soul to the glory of God. The key word now was not get; instead it was and is *receive*. This union with God revives the soul, bringing it to the use God intended; my soul would now operate in fellowship with the Holy Spirit's life in me. As David wrote, "He restoreth my soul." (Psalm 23:3, KJV)

As I came to know and understand these truths, my addiction to soul experiences began to fall away; the intense striving after them eased. The pressure to get more and more waned. I could still have soul experiences and indeed did, many and beautiful, but they were no longer the goal of my life; I no longer felt driven by them. The chase, it appeared, had ended, the ravenous craving had been quenched by the beauty and person of Jesus. Instead I learned to receive with gladness and gratitude to God when he gave soul refreshments.

The Spirit now orchestrated experiences that engaged my soul. While not always as charged with titanic excitement, these experiences were actually more deeply moving and satisfying. That is easy to write, but hard to define. I admit freely that the sense of experiencing something glorious and incredible and sometimes mind shattering was no longer as frequent as it had been. My experiences at that time now had far deeper meaning and far greater relevance to the fabric of living. These commonplace experiences gave and continue to give incredible purpose to my being and to my living. To pray with another, to render an act of kindness, to look with love and compassion into another's heart, to enable a person to know and understand the love of God, to invite another to salvation in Christ, to intercede as I shared God's heart for the hurting: these have become the crowning moments of life. They occur in quietness usually, and are lacking in fanfare. But how can I relate their true significance? I cannot. Here's the point: I can now receive "soul experiences" but not be driven to define my life by them, and I find them in the ordinary days of my life as the Holy Spirit opens them to me.

I had come to firmly believe and experience this before the onset of my illness. I truly believed that I was led by the Spirit of God into this new realm of soul experience. But this awareness grew far more acute after my fall and the onset of nephritis when I could no longer "go after" the big thrill. It was then I discovered in dismay how much my soul *rather than* the Holy Spirit sought to rule in my life! Now in this transition time, both soul and spirit seemed diminished, and I was resentful of it. Nothing satisfied much; all seemed rather shallow and mundane. Sometimes a glimmer of truth excited me; sometimes a song stirred my heart; sometimes a sunrise brought delight. Mostly I felt flat. Tired. Unmoved.

I had thought that I was fully submitted to the Spirit, but now I wanted back lovely spectacles and happy outings and exciting travel. I wanted to dance and sing and go to parties. Resorting to seeking soul experiences to brighten up my dull, dull days, I again began to claim them as my right; I felt entitled to have them. I began to insist that the abundant life was a life of good times and blessings and that these were my "rights." In the dullness of disease, I began to seek soul experiences to fill the void since I now had few spiritually led experiences and outlets. Where was the music that could stir me, the pictures of nature that could move me, the films that would rend my emotions, the fall foliage that would make me feel alive again? I needed soul stimulation! But it wasn't immensely satisfying when I got it. Not if I pursued it and felt I had to have it. Oddly enough, I was much better off if I just received it as God gave it as a good gift now and then, as he had previously taught me to do. He still knew and does know what will feed both my spirit and soul. I don't have to become a "taker" again.

I frankly see in myself and in other elderly people this longing to feed on soul experiences as the greatest temptation in old age. Who has not met the person that reminisces endlessly about past deeds and exploits? Who tries to recapture the glory? Who still sees himself or herself as the champion? Who can't let you forget that it was better then, more noble, more valiant, or more exciting, colorful, fashionable, stylish, or more of a contribution, an achievement, a stroke of genius? The past is the triumph; the rose color never fades. The one remembering lives on past dreams—that is life's greatest value, always told with something of a sigh and a lament. I find this sad and quite short of life as the Lord meant us to have it, even in old age. It is a grasping after.

There is certainly a time for wonderful memories. When they come, joy and gratitude for the richness God has given rise in a chorus of praise. But these are not trophies to be endlessly displayed and bragged about. I later had an unusual experience of just such memories which I will explain in Part II.

The elder also deals with the temptation to prolong youth. This is the old person who will not admit to ageing, and must prove by amount of activity or vigor of it that nothing really has changed in his or her ability to do the amazing feats of middle age, to still do all and receive the admiring and animated compliments of the on-lookers. (I think I have just described the "pre-fall" me!) While I have surely tried this myself, and basked in the glory at the time, I found it again a thing of pride and vanity, a pressure to perform. Somehow I knew I was grasping after admiration as my main motivation. And somehow, I realized I was "past it" and trying too hard. The soul apart from the Spirit's leading will not give up its godhood willingly. And thus a satisfying time of life in the here and now is forfeited.

I am certainly for as much activity as is possible for the elderly or diminished person. It is wonderful to continue joyous activities as long as possible, and a boon to health as well. It is the over-achievement (tip-toeing over slippery logs) that finds us out, that shows our true motivation to remain forever young—when we aren't. Hard facts!

If not these, consider those who must have the enriched retirement with endless golf, or parties or card playing, or new lessons in line dancing or lawn bowling or garden clubbing. Not that any of these are wrong in themselves; they are not. Nor is becoming a champion of social causes or political involvement or new contributions to social betterment. Some may indeed be just what the Lord is asking us to do for needed exercise and involvement with unbelievers. But if they are meant to provide the major purpose and meaning to this time of life, I find they fail. But if they do, the soul rules, not God. And the abundant life in Christ is missed.

When the cry of the heart is, "I am now worthless. What can I do? How can I be valuable again?" it is very distressing to the one crying; I know this from experience. But the answer will not be found in the soul's quest for renewed glory or even filling. It instead induces the cry of "Vanity, vanity, all is vanity," with resulting desperation and depression. Where is meaning then, and purpose in this last mile home?

In my early days of diminishment, it was not my soul that needed "feeding"; it was my spirit. I found more and more that the Lord was showing me not to seek after even good soul experiences, that he would give those when and if he chose. I was instead to seek to dwell in my spirit with him in the experiences he would give. I found him speaking new and profound messages in the Scripture. When I lingered with him, I found myself learning and growing still in spiritual realms in dialogue with him, in times of sheer abiding, being "at home" with him, of learning just to be in his presence. I found he would direct in the books he brought to me. He would direct me in bringing people into my life. He showed me the Scriptures, teaching me how to dwell in them, meditate on them, consider their applications and messages. Clearly, I needed to feast on the fellowship of the Lord himself for my deepest needs. He, if I walked in the Spirit, would "restore my soul," leading me into the activities he ordained for me.

How contrary this is to the world where soul power reigns as the religion of choice. True believers in it seek one grand new experience after another, one new success after another, one new ultimate experience after another as a meaningful way of living. Then one day perhaps there is a waking up to the core of emptiness of spirit, and a plaintive asking, "Is this all there is?"

One night George and I watched "American Experience" on TV. It featured the life of silent film star Mary Pickford. What a tragedy to watch Mary gradually lose her career as she aged and in doing so, lose all that meant anything to her, to assuage her grief with drink, to divorce her husband, to try to branch out and fail, to end up a sad recluse. Truly, what shall it profit a woman if she gains the whole world and loses her soul?

I thought clearly again that life as given by God is meant to be lived in the spiritual union of my spirit with the Holy Spirit, and that life invades all other life in me, my soul and my body. When this is my state, then my soul is safe to expand under the Spirit's gifting and direction. And expand it does in ways I could never have foreseen. Then I do not make my soul my god, an idol to be worshipped. Then God can take the beauty and wonder of the soul as well as the body and mold it and enlarge it and give it incredible grace for his own use. Then he can give it away into his love of people.

What I discovered in my transition into old age is that the soul, led by the Spirit, can actually become more vibrant and beautiful and useful to God, enlarged to go deeper and higher and wider and longer than ever before in a spirit realm beyond end. For now there is time along the road for this process to occur. There is now time to *linger* and *receive* on this road of diminishment.

CHAPTER EIGHT

ANOTHER TIME

L inger. What an apt word: to pause and ponder and drink in the essence of a place, a happening, a person, a thought, a wonder of life. When I linger, there is time for me to see and experience in many ways the incredible beauty that God designed for us to know. This new sense of unpressured time was not foreign to me before my diminishment, for I had sought it from time to time, but neither was it the pace at which I usually moved. I would need to learn to live in this new time zone far more frequently if I wanted to walk in step with God this last mile home.

I learned from the writings of my pastor, Mark Buchanan, two Greek words for time and the differences in their meanings. It was quite a revelation. Here is his explanation from his book *The Rest of God*:

> The first word is *chronos*—familar to us because it's the root of
> many of our own words: *chronology, chronicle, chronic.* It is the time

of clock and calendar, time as a gauntlet, time as a forced march.
The word derives from one of the gods in the Greek pantheon,
Chronos was a nasty minor deity, a glutton and a cannibal who
gorged himself on his own children. He was always consuming,
never consummated . . . Chronos is the presiding deity of the
driven.

The second Greek word is *kairos*. This is time as gift, as opportunity, as season. It is time pregnant with purpose. In *kairos* time you
ask, not "What time is it?" but "What is this time *for*?" *Kairos* is the
servant of holy purpose. "There is a time for everything," Ecclesiastes
says, "and a season for every activity under heaven."[2]

That beautifully clarifies the meanings of these time concepts for me.

I remember too well being "eaten up" by time. When I was in my
thirties and forties I joked that I hit the floor running in order to do all
that needed to be done in a day, especially when I had three children to
get off to school and baby-sitter, my teaching job to get to and perform,
groceries to buy, food to cook, kitchen to clean, kids to bathe, clothes
to ready for the next day's wear, lessons to prepare, bedtime rituals, and
various and sundry other tasks to perform as need arose. When the
teaching year ended, I became the orchard attendant for our grove of
five hundred apple trees, hastening back and forth all day to the house
and orchard, then harvesting the produce, preparing it for sale, then
assisting in the sale of it. My schedule was as packed as a mountaineer's
backpack.

In the years after I became a counselor, I continued a packed schedule,
balancing personal needs with counseling appointments and pursuit of
my profession. Sometimes I scheduled in a day or half-day for visiting
the realm of *kairos* time. Occasionally I entered in gladly and fully. I
wrote a poem on one such day along the California coast:

Sea Sabbath

I sit on the bluff above a vast ocean
Sea sapphire this day.
Before me, centered, is molten silver.
White diamonds spread outward,
Mirror magic of a thinly clouded sun.
Breakers surge and mount,
Grow green in the turning,
Tumble into milky froth
that stretches forth
Slow,
Sweeps the sand,
Retreats and disappears.
Caught in the sight and endless sound,
Held by hypnotic force,
I melt into mere being.
Time ends here on the brink of the world.

Not that my visits to the realm of *kairos* were as frequent as I wished. I pledged to have more when I retired. But habits are strong, so when I retired at sixty-five, I really didn't. Having moved to British Columbia, I just kept on with the habits I had grown used to, particularly a tightly packed schedule. I felt guilty of laziness if I didn't have it fairly well crammed. George and I rearranged the house, spruced up the walls, the yard, the flower bed, planned wonderfully packed trips—and took them, square danced and round danced and attended every Seniors dance, filling the days full. Church became paramount, so in time I taught classes, did volunteer counseling, trained lay counselors and prayer counselors, and served on boards and committees. (I also managed to write a book.) I can honestly say I thought I had it all balanced beautifully along with our marriage, home duties, family, and friends. Proud of my ability to schedule it all, I kept everything in its slot, with no time wasted. A tight schedule to be sure, but I must admit that at the time I thought it just right.

What I realize now is that I was habitually driven by *chronos* about 90% of the time. Underneath it all lay my hidden belief that one must be busy to be valuable. I would never have admitted that until everything in my life came to a standstill. Then I saw clearly the dimensions of time in my life and the extent to which my schedule had ruled me. Now I learned my *chronos* tyranny by its absence. Yet I felt lost without my schedule, aimless, purposeless, and wanting back my time prison. I felt anxious and at loose ends. My inner clock kept on ticking, and a sense of urgency went with it. An inner voice kept saying, "All right, now that is done. Now what's next? Get on with it!"

For some, a schedule is exactly what they need, and the Lord is asking them to establish and to follow one. But for me my schedule had become a tyranny of habit wrongly motivated, and I knew he was insisting that it end.

I had liked to think, before the big stop, that I embraced *kairos* frequently, and indeed there were those times I slowed or paused and just drank in the beauty, the wonder, the meaning behind, the transcendent, willing myself to receive the special moment when experience took on new depths of awareness, meaning, aliveness. When I grasped after such moments, they eluded me. When they came to me, I was blessed, drawn past my rational self, and longing for more. I often considered what it would take to obtain these jewels of time. I really didn't know then and didn't have time to find out! I had too many important things on my plate, and if I didn't keep to my schedule I would never accomplish them. And I must do them, mustn't I? How was I to include *kairos* experience? Now I know.

As I said, I now have few *chronos* time pressures. When I came to a full stop, every time pressure dropped away. Not driven now, I was still left with that inexplicable anxiety because of it. I realized I now had the time to go slowly and to receive life more fully and deeply, and I wanted to. But my old habits inhibited me. I found myself trying to set up a schedule again because I simply felt the comfort and security of it, as well as the curtailment of the underlying anxiety. For without constant use of my time in a scheduled, goal oriented form, I felt my life had no meaning. What was I without accomplishment?

Taking the medications prescribed, then feeling better, I began to sense the need to do more and to re-establish scheduling to make it possible. But I felt a distinct check in my spirit. (Later, as my energy nose-dived, I realized I couldn't have kept it up if I had wanted to!) As I grasped these concepts of time from Mark's book, I came to realize my need of a major overhaul in my thinking and habits regarding schedules. How could the old compulsive habits be broken? As I confessed to God and asked him for wisdom to realize when I began to "do it again," my awareness became acute. Sometimes I wanted *not* to be aware; I wanted to just go ahead and get something done; I wanted . . . I wanted . . . I wanted. Well, of course I had a choice. I could stop and listen to God, or I could go on. The battle raged, and I didn't find easy victory. But I did begin to choose to stop; I know that's when the Lord's enablement to do so became apparent. The listening to him—now that was another hard choice. I knew I would need then to sit quietly in the Lord's presence and begin to realize his peace and his pace, to step into them, to walk in them in union with him. He would guide me into what to do and when to do it. What a process! Beyond my choice to stop, this required discipline and practice.

I had lots of questions. When, like Mary, I choose to sit in quietness at the feet of Jesus and really listen to him, what may I come to realize? What may be revealed to me? What will happen when I give long moments to whole new awareness of life and experience that he wants to give? What will I come to know of him, the wonder and richness of his presence?

I now continue to meet with the Lord each morning, first for worship and fellowship, and then to ask him what he would have me to do that day. I seek to walk the day slowly, keeping in his presence, continuing our dialogue, relishing fellowship, and giving time to the *kairos* experiences as they present themselves. I long to give him delight, as he delights me.

These considerations have brought me to long to experience this *kairos* of the Holy Spirit more fully. I have asked the Lord to reveal its full meaning to me. I'm not there, but I am learning. Life has surely become richer because of it.

> You have made known to me the path of life;
> you will fill me with joy in your presence,
> with eternal pleasures at your right hand. (Psalm 16:11)

One of the greatest of these riches, these pleasures, is what I am experiencing with persons. As a counselor I often listened intensely to a person in order to discern what was happening in the inner being. I not only wanted to ease the pain, to gain clarity, to give hope; I wanted to solve the problem. On *kairos* time, my encounter is not goal oriented. In no hurry and with no set agenda, I can now listen receptively with the Lord's love flowing toward that person in me with no divided heart. I find I am enabled to know and appreciate the person, to love with my full heart, to receive awareness of the fullness of God's handiwork in that unique being. Often far deeper insights come than just solving the problem. Pleasure and joy in loving are present even when I empathize with the person's sorrow.

I like to invite a friend to have lunch with me at a place in Duncan called the Garage. They serve delicious soups. Or to come have tea with me in my home. Or iced tea on the patio. As we eat or drink, I love to experience the conversation develop and unfold; I desire just to take in the person I'm with. I long to sense that friend *whole*, with all the uniqueness of design and appearance, eye expression, voice tones, gestures, emotions, and yes, words that I open myself to receive. In essence, to see with the eyes and heart of God. What pleasure. What riches. Here lie the depths I have longed to reach, not evident on the surface but full of unseen currents and flow.

Another great blessing of living in kairos time is opening up to me now. I find myself still and silent enough to open to times of prolonged meditation. Scripture has long been a treasure trove of words to be pondered, but now I wait longer in expectation that the Spirit will reveal more insights and new awareness. How fruitful this has been for me. Passages I have long known now seem new in the richness of meditation: words, images, and characters hold new dimensions.

Then there are those times when I find myself meditating on ordinary daily thoughts or memories. One day I recalled the years of my early childhood when we had to draw water for household use from an outside well. How clearly I saw my mother at that well, letting down the bucket, hearing the splash, drawing up that cold clear water, laboring to balance it as she carried it into the kitchen. It was a treat to drink a dipperful of that fresh water, spilling some on myself for a quick cooling on a hot day. At times, though, that well contained only gravelly impure water. It was a shallow well and lacked the depth necessary during prolonged dry seasons to maintain volume and purity. Then we'd have to ask our neighbors to use their deep well. Theirs did not "run dry" as ours did. At any time you could draw up the clear sweet water we all craved—abundant water and gladly given. Someone in years past had known the importance of digging deep, a work that took great will and effort, but paid off generously in times of need.

How true, I thought, of one's relationship to God. Time, effort, will, perseverance—all are required in abundance if one is to maintain a deep well. My thoughts lingered on this, Spirit taught and deeply satisfying.

I long to learn more and more of *kairos* time with the Lord, fully entering into it with him. I know how easy it is to drift back into driven and pressured ways, to be eaten up again by *chronos*. So I pray to learn to linger with Christ, to listen more closely, to become ever more aware of life in him this last mile home.

CHAPTER NINE

LOVING KINDNESS

I picked up my "old" Bible and began reading in the Psalms. My old Bible was the New American Standard Bible, a translation I had used extensively in teaching Bible studies over thirty years ago. In those years, to begin our time together each week, we women, about sixty to eighty of us, often sang choruses that were based on the Psalms. As I reminisced, I read Psalm 63. Verse 3 electrified my thinking:

> Because Thy lovingkindness is better than life,
>> My lips will praise Thee.
> So I will bless Thee as long as I live;
>> I will lift up my hands in Thy name.

The chorus I had so often sung in those past years based on that Psalm now began singing in my mind. Memories of that time flooded back. I lingered in them awhile, seeing again the young, earnest women we were, loving again the dear friends of those years, their beautiful faces worshipping the God they loved.

Gradually the memories faded, replaced by my big *now.* Then strong questions filled my mind: What does this mean, that his lovingkindness is better than life? Better than what life? What is this lovingkindness?

I knew this word in Hebrew; it is *hesed* (or *chesed*). I began to ponder again and research it to discover the answers to my questions.

In Hosea 2:19, 20, God tells Israel:

> "And I will betroth you to Me forever;
> Yes, I will betroth you to Me in righteousness and in justice.
> In lovingkindness and in compassion.
> And I will betroth you to Me in faithfulness.
> Then you will know the Lord."

There is an editor's note in the Ryrie Study Bible (NASB) that explains:

"lovingkindness. The Hebrew word is *hesed,* used about 250 times in the O. T. It means loyal, steadfast, or faithful love and stresses the idea of belonging together of those involved in the love relationship. Here it connotes God's faithful love for his unfaithful people." Then follows a listing of other references where this word is used, especially in the Minor Prophets. This note continues: "In the O. T., communion, deliverance, enablement, enlightenment, guidance, forgiveness, hope, praise, preservation are all based on God's *hesed.*"[3]

I read the words over and and over. Are these true for me now? Do I experience from God all of these: Communion? Enlightenment? Guidance? Forgiveness? Hope? Praise? Preservation? If so, in what measure? Do I find this lovingkindness of God in my life now? How is it better than life? How can that be?

A dear friend of mine, Lynda Kinnee, loaned me a book by Malcolm Smith entitled *The Lost Secret of the New Covenant.* In it the author first gives the history of how God formed a covenant with Israel. Concerning *hesed*, he explains, "It is a word rich with meaning, but at its heart it describes the mutual responsibilities that each party to a covenant has to the other, and the rights that each enjoys in the covenant relationship."[4]

I looked up a listing of this word translated "lovingkindness" in my Young's Concordance, focusing on it in the Psalms. I decided to use this word, lovingkindness, as a meditation in coming days. How, I asked the Lord, could these aspects of his relating to me now be better than life itself? Did he extend this lovingkindness to his New Covenant children as he had to the Israelites? How did I now experience his *hesed*? Did I truly find it better than life? How did that translate into my experience? I decided to take one reference a day and meditate on it in regard to these questions. In days that followed my eyes were increasingly opened, my mind enlightened, with more and more understanding of the true nature of God. Here are a few of my entries.

My journal records my thoughts of Psalm 17: 7, 8:

> Wondrously show Thy lovingkindness,
>> O Savior of those who take refuge at Thy right hand
> From those who rise up against them.
> Keep me as the apple of the eye;
>> Hide me in the shadow of Thy wings.

"This is the place of God's incredible cherishing of David, of love and protection, of deep, personal relationship. Isn't this the exact picture God has given to me of how he loves, cherishes, and relates to me personally? Isn't a love relationship like this beyond mere life? What do I have in this relationship with God?"

From Psalm 40: "Verse 11, 'Thy lovingkindness and Thy truth will continually preserve me.' In this psalm David speaks of his iniquities being more than the hairs of his head. But these and his fears, 'my heart has failed,' will not prevent God's lovingkindness from preserving him.

God preserves David because his love kindly does so. This is mercy. The merciful God acts to preserve him—and me. I don't deserve God's preserving me; I deserve the opposite. What a sense of entitlement to life, abundance, well-being, praise, and love I have maintained! Truth—It is all God's mercy, his lovingkindness to me that he forgives and preserves me." I was struck again, and with force, by the incredible graciousness of God to man, and to me personally, considering the sinful life I had lived, that God extended mercy to me in an ever flowing stream.

This theme reverberates again in Psalm 51:1:

> Be gracious to me, O God,
>> according to Thy lovingkindness;
> According to the greatness of
>> Thy compassion blot out my transgressions.

My journal comments:

> Here God's great compassion is identified with his lovingkindness. The *hesed* flows from the great heart of compassion . . . He bends to be gracious. David now realizes how very sinful he has been—adultery, murder, lying—and he is smitten with the realization that nothing can be fixed, redeemed, or restored unless he offers to God the sacrifice of a 'broken spirit; a broken and contrite heart . . . .'

O great mercy of God, O great compassionate heart that does blot out our transgressions and then creates in us a clean heart. We know that God forgives, but do we realize the fullness of His lovingkindness that extends it?"

Psalm 48:9, and 1, 2: (In this psalm the singer is extolling God for Zion, that is, Jerusalem.)

> We have thought on Thy lovingkindess, O God,
>> In the midst of Thy temple.
> In the city of our God, His holy mountain.
> Beautiful in elevation, the joy of the whole earth,
>> Is Mount Zion in the far north,

The city of the great King. God, in her palaces,
Has made Himself known as a stronghold.

I meditated on God's lovingkindness shown by his chosen dwelling place. "What love he shows to dwell there among his people. And what is his temple, his dwelling place now? I am. Every believer is. As Zion to the Jew so is the throne room of God to me. What love, what grace, that he has chosen to dwell there!"

Another entry in my journal continues this theme:

I awoke today first to Psalm 5 and found:

But as for me by Thy abundant lovingkindness
I will enter Thy house . . .

Here I see David coming into the temple. How excellent that he knew it was only by the great grace and mercy of God that he was allowed to enter and enjoy the presence and relationship of God.

How true it is for me, Lord. You give yourself to me to enter your fellowship, your presence today. How blessed I am. Your company is the great prize.

'How kind of you to let me come,' says Eliza Doolittle in her vocal exercise (remember *My Fair Lady?*). How true! How kind of you to let me come. How gracious you are. How inviting. How welcoming. How joyous to be with me. How marvelous for me to *rest in* before being *led out!*

I am learning the deep wells of peace and joy.

I found another theme in Psalm 86:5:

For Thou, O Lord, art good, and ready to forgive
And abundant in lovingkindness to all who call upon Thee.

In my journal, I wrote,

Here again is that picture of God just *waiting* to bestow all he wants to give. What releases it? It is released to 'all who call upon Thee.' I can just picture a child pulling off a shirt. He gets stuck with it when it is upside down over his face. All his struggles make it worse. At last he cries for help. What a pleasure it is to the parent to free him, calm him, comfort him, laugh with him—that's lovingkindness, a moment not to be missed—and not forgotten. Why do we resist God's loving-kindness? Why do we not call upon him? I remember an old commercial on TV; the frustrated daughter says indignantly to her mother, who is trying to assist her, 'Puleeese, Mother, I'd rather do it myself!' How much joy with God do we miss with this attitude?

In regard to Psalm 69, I wrote:

David is drowning in a quagmire of despondency, a pit of despair; he is sure his enemies are going to destroy him. He has been dishonored and reproached, made a laughing-stock, a by-word. He is appealing to God that God in his lovingkindness would draw him out. In verse 13, he cries,

O God, in the greatness of Thy lovingkindness
  Answer me with Thy saving truth.

Truth can rescue! O God, tell me the truth, your truth, and it will lead me out of my pit, draw me up and out. I see as I am open to this loving truth, I am instructed, corrected, led, lifted.

Verse 16:

Thy lovingkindness is good.
According to the greatness of Thy compassion, turn to me . . .

Compassion is a great component of lovingkindness. God sees his children with pity for their weak state, for their plight. Even when I have foolishly followed my own way, his compassion would draw me out, lead me back. How precious then to me are both the thoughts and the feelings of God.

One of my favorites as I continued my meditations was Psalm 143. The entire psalm brought me into depths of reflection. I wrote:

> David experienced his enemies constantly, unremittingly hounding him, crushing him to the ground (verse 3). He knew he could not appeal to God to save him on the basis of his personal righteousness (verse 2)—he wasn't righteous and he knew it! It was God who was full of faithfulness and righteousness (verse 1). So his appeal for deliverance is to God's lovingkindness:
>
> > Let me hear Thy lovingkindness in the morning
> > For I trust in Thee;
> > Teach me the way in which I should walk;
> > For to Thee I lift up my soul (verse 8)

And in verse 12:

> > And in Thy lovingkindness
> > cut off my enemies . . . (verse 12)

I added:

> I have been appealing to God on the basis of *my* past doings, not God's. I have been saying, 'Look what I have done! Look at what I yet can do!' Oh, let me come, as David did, to consider the marvel of what *God* has done, what God can do, what God is about. Oh let me thirst after my God! Let me fully realize you, Lord God, what you are doing, what you desire. Let me walk in your train, always beholding you. You are the wonder, the glorious One.

Then I admonished myself:

> See Jesus only. Behold, hear, touch, watch, attend. Join his adventure. Be where he is. Stop telling him to come to you. Join him.

During this period I meditated on many more passages, day by day. Each morning I found myself eager to find the next installment in the "lovingkindness" saga. When I was a child I listened to daily radio serials.

Jerry and I would race home from school each day, perch ourselves in the corner of the kitchen, and glue our ears to the next incredible adventures of the Green Hornet, Jack Armstrong, and the Lone Ranger. I had this same feeling of exciting discovery in these meditations of Scripture.

One day an incredible realization swept over me: my loving God was pouring out, raining down, deluging me with *lovingkindness* every moment of every day—in the light that filled the skies, in the air I breathed, in all the ways small and large that my life was maintained moment by moment, in the safety I experienced wherever I went, in the water I drank, in the foods I ate, in the clothes I wore, in the house I lived, in the sights, sounds, smells, touches and tastes continually, in the workings of my organs and my brain, in my spirit and soul and body, in the creation around me—every leaf, flower, cloud, stream, and in all the people of my life, every smile, every nod, every touch, every kindness. And on and on it rained, pure *hesed*. I couldn't isolate or name the goodnesses fast enough; it was all just that steady, unending, never failing flood of lovingkindnesss pouring on me. It was love unbounded, free flowing, unsought, unasked for, and so unheeded. If this was earth, what would heaven be, where no sin mars sight or awareness, where nothing obscures? I sat in silence and marveled. How was it I hadn't noticed? How was it I hadn't fully realized? "Ah, forgive me," I cried to God, even as I knew unspeakable joy rising within me. I felt a myriad voices inside beginning to sing like a choir of angels raising soaring anthems of praise and unending thanksgiving.

At length I began to walk through my day. But realms of gratitude had been awakened in me beyond any I had ever known. It was the beginning of realizing the meaning of those incredible words, "Thy lovingkindness is better than life."

I tried to sum up my understanding in my journal:

> The *hesed* of God: the love of God that is a total thing. It unites all

God's being to focus on man with the intention to bless him, to benefit him, and to draw him into relationship with the God who gives. It is the heart, mind, and will of God united in giving. It is length, breadth, depth, and height. It is exceedingly abundantly above all we ask or think. It is constant, unseen, and mostly unacknowledged. It is all mercy and grace. It is the rain that falls on the just and the unjust. It is light, love, and life rolled into one. It is the unceasing father/ mother care of God.

This theme of *hesed* continued to fill my mind and heart, but not just in my quiet times of meditation. Many times during the day, my awareness of it would come suddenly. Sipping a cup of hot chocolate, I'd say to myself exultantly, "*Hesed.* Pure *hesed.*" I would feel silly and smile and then realize: Jesus was smiling too.

Having become aware of *hesed* in its many aspects, I was now able to have a heightened awareness of those things I encountered day by day. Small things drew my focus and with a deeper look came appreciation. My senses became more focused and acute; I became more engrossed in textures, colors, tastes, fragrances, details of design and fabric and contour. I became more aware of all that I saw in people: their eyes and all the expressions of them, facial features, mouths, teeth, voice tone and texture, body tone and posture, and many other subtle messages given out unconsciously. I lingered.

Later I moved to meditations on other subjects. Yet nothing has erased or diminished the impact of these meditations on the *hesed* of God; it is a realm in which I delight to live, knowing, as I have begun to learn, that his lovingkindness is better than life.

CHAPTER TEN

PEACE AND PLAY

As I have been describing, the re-orienting of my thinking and walking with Jesus, at his pace, into my day has changed many things. One very meaningful change I welcomed greatly was staying in his peace. When I am in union with Jesus, I am filled with the peace I see in him, an indescribable assurance, authority, calm, yet vibrant life. As has often been said, he is "unworried, unhurried." I would stay in this place of peace always. But I don't. I have learned to enter it more frequently, though, since my diminishment.

The biggest block to this peace was, and often still is, my habit of anxiety. I have had a life-long habit of moving as my anxiety has pressured me to move, and now I began to be conscious of it. The Lord was making it clear—if I was to have his peace, this habit must go; it was fear; it was unfaith; it was sin. I wanted to be rid of it. I couldn't do it though—I became anxious just thinking about it! I was bred on anxiety as my chapter on fear describes—my fears at five were huge, introverted, and prolonged, producing habits of worry and anxiety that became first thoughts in almost every situation.

I think most of us can sense anxiety in others. We sense their fear. We intuit their drivenness. We sense their push to control or their uncomfortable ill-at-easeness. You know, how in those moments of silence, your mind goes utterly blank and you cannot think of *one* thing to say, not one, and neither can the other person. Feeling all that tension, we react with our own anxiety, knowing these things exist in us too. But we've all grown used to it; it's just the way life is in these days of technology and terrestrial change.

In the summer of 2006, George and I were going to travel to Leavenworth, Washington, to join my sister Rose and her husband Doug for a few days there for the kind of fun we have only with those two. We looked forward to it very much, so we planned plenty of time to travel and to arrive in the afternoon of the day Rose and Doug would arrive in the evening. Only one problem: On my planner calendar I wrote down their arrival a day later than the one they planned! So while we were blithely traveling our way toward them, they had already arrived the evening before, were on the lookout for us, and getting more and more worried by the hour. More than that, we had forgotten to take our cell phone.

Where were we? Why weren't we there? Horrible possibilities bombarded them.

Having spent a night of anxious sleep, they were now, at mid-day, feeling something near all-out panic. They called the Highway Patrol, telephoned hospitals, checked with my neighbor, called my pastor and his wife, Cheryl, who is one of my very closest friends, and even asked her to go over to my house and check to see if I was somehow still there.

(She did; I wasn't.) While Doug made calls, Rose kept a constant watch on the parking lot at the motel. No answers. No arrivals.

The fires of intense worry burned out of control.

Finally we arrived, very surprised to see them in the parking lot waiting for us! My sister ran to me in tears shouting, "Oh praise God! Praise God!" She threw her arms around me, clutching, crying, trembling, and asking me repeatedly what had happened that we were so late. Our disjointed dialogue unraveled the whole story. Ah, how crushing to perceive that my carelessness was the cause of all this suffering!

Now I never in my life want to cause any person that kind of worry again.

So now when we are going to have a rendezvous with Rose and Doug, I write down the date, check it at least twice, write it down two more times, and then get anxious. Did I get it right? Did I write it down correctly? Have I somehow messed up again? I check some more. Finally, I realize I am working myself into a frenzy of worry. I confess this to the Lord and then rest in the decision to now leave this in his hands, having done all that I should do, and asking him to lead me into anything further that needs to be done. I rest down then and realize I really do not have to do penance in order to have peace.

George was to have his eighty-fifth birthday in early April of 2008. Considering my poor health, he declined the idea of a grand party and chose a convenient reception instead. So we planned to serve cake with tea and coffee to the congregation after second service at our church. After we talked it over, I began immediately to make plans for it: I asked a lady from the church to prepare the cake, then I booked the room we'd need, and then I began to list the other things I would need to provide, such as plates, napkins, forks, and an extensive picture display.

Then came that anxious feeling spurred by anxious questions: what am I forgetting? how will it all come together? will the people like the cake? what should we put cards in? how can we control the children who come back for seconds and thirds? will there be enough cake? etc., etc. Some of these things could be easily addressed; some couldn't. But the moment I began to be anxious, I knew I was walking toward the pit. Right away I began lamenting my weakened condition; I no longer had the strength to undertake this. I knew that in my illness and weakness, I was more forgetful than ever. But what was I to do? I *must* see it through, mustn't I? I'd best push on. I could not afford anxiety!

Suddenly understanding dawned—it was not my weakness but my anxiety that was sapping my strength! "Be anxious for nothing, but in everything by prayer . . . " (Phil. 4:6) filled my mind. I ran into the throne room, fell into God's arms, and had a good cry over it all. How blessed to be received, heard, forgiven, and caught up into the love and peace of the Lord. My head cleared. I asked him for guidance on items that truly needed to be addressed. I listened and received the guidance I needed, then left the rest with him and refused to worry about it. I was at peace again.

We had a lovely and happy and stress free reception. Several wonderful people pitched in to help and to cut the cake. No one had ever seen a cake so long (almost 4 feet) and so uniquely decorated, a picture of a Spitfire on one end and a picture of a dancing couple on the other, the one George's fondest memory—flying his plane—and the other his favorite pastime, dancing. More than one hundred people sang a rousing "Happy Birthday," ate cake, and peered at the picture gallery along the side of the room: of George, the child, the WW2 pilot, the fisherman, the hunter, the Junior Forest Warden of Alberta, the glad father, the friend and buddy, the traveler, the dancer, the happy husband. The kids had all they wanted, and still there was cake left. George was delighted. I was exhausted afterwards, true. But I had not been anxious!

Sadly I find my habit of anxiety still rises frequently, manifesting itself in a sense of urgency. I often awaken with a sense that I have something important to do, and for the life of me, I cannot remember what. I can only feel that uneasiness that motivates me to hurry through my day, lest I suddenly remember my assignment, and find I do not have time to complete it. It is like a bad dream. I am learning to curtail this as the Lord has taught me: with the first awareness of my anxious feelings, I am to stop and take those thoughts captive, release them to him and let go, resting in his love and peace. After awhile I ask for and then listen quietly to his instructions. Then I can move into action with him. From pit to peace!

I'd rather not feel anxiety at all. With diminishment, at first I had much more. But now, having practiced the prayer that brings me to release, I truly have far less. I don't go far enough if I just release anxiety to him; I must also put on his peace.

Another anxiety I came to realize lay under my relationships to people. I have always been incredibly afraid of not pleasing. Why is Momma frowning? Why are those girls looking at me that way? Why is the teacher so cross today? What put Daddy in that foul temper? Why is my boyfriend flirting with that other girl? What is wrong with me? What have I done? Why don't they like me? Why do they make fun of me? The pain of disapproval, of rejection, of indifference pierced deep, creating chronic wounds and deep scar tissue. The wounding became worse, direct and intentional, life-threatening, more painful than I could ever have imagined, and longer lasting. I learned an array of self-protective skills, totally necessary if I was to continue living.

Still I wanted to be truly loving and loved, but by now I was afraid to allow myself to be truly known. Though my deep love of Jesus and he for me began the long process of healing my wounds, I did not release some of my self protection. I came in time to love people again, and to long to bring them the love I had found in the Lord.

This led in time to my training to become a counselor. And counsel I did, for almost thirty years, ever seeking to perfect my skills, to be more effective. What a wonderfully hidden place to be. I could love and give and never be in danger of it becoming truly reciprocal. It didn't work for personal relationships, of course, though I couldn't see it at the time. Through long bouts of more personal pain and learning, I finally saw myself truly. In my journal I wrote,

> What I am realizing is that I have long loved people intentionally—I have accepted them as they are, refused to judge them while clearly discerning faults, sinfulness, shallowness, pretence, and have sought to reveal to them the genuine love of Jesus for their needs. (All very important in counseling.) What I have not done in Jesus is *receive* them. Accepted, not received. I think by this I mean I have not welcomed each one's unique being into a heart of love, and given them a home there. I have let them walk around the 'outside of my house' and treated them with respect, but I have not let them, hurtful as they might turn out to be, come into the inner chambers and be received as persons made in God's image to find a *home* in me. Not just mere cordiality or welcome to show my goodness and magnitude, but with a genuine receiving. This means I risk the willingness to be truly known and loved myself. I must dwell deep in the heart of Christ himself for this to truly happen. Otherwise the woman at the well, the leper, the prostitute, the tax collector will never know that love—nor will I as lover and beloved. Vastly new learning for me, Jesus; bold and risky. I have received God's enormous lovingkindness towards me. Now he, in me, would play it forward to everyone he 'allows' me, instructs me, directs me to connect with. I yearn to know this flow fully.

This willingness to know and be known, to love and be loved, has not only brought closure to much of my anxiety, but blessed me immeasurably. Revealing an openness and transparency of my person, I am relaxed and real, unguarded and not anxious. I don't say I am always liked, but I am myself. And at peace.

I have written about my anxiety that arose from my loss of ministry, impacting my sense of self-worth. The Lord provided a wonderful antidote to this particular kind of anxiety; he led me to be playful. By playful I mean an attitude of heart and mind as well as action. In my journal I wrote, "I must allow him to end my anxiety. ' . . . unless you are converted, and become like children, you shall not enter the kingdom of heaven.' ' . . . the way is narrow that leads to life, and few are those who find it.' 'Abide in Me . . . ' 'These things I have spoken unto you that My joy may be in you, and that your joy may be full' (all quotes NASB). God speaks to me through these verses about childlikeness of trust and confidence. *Trust* this leading. Give yourself over to him for joyous adventure, as a child would a parent. Exchange old age for a childhood of spirit! Engage in the freedom of the child, the playfulness of the child, the timelessness of the child, the wonder and delight of the child, the love of the child for the parent/friend." Laughter, frequent and familiar, comes readily; I sing and dance more vigorously, if only in my heart. Hello King David; may I join you in the worship parade?

Anxiety for most of us is so familiar that we do not recognize we have it; it just rides our backs in regard to almost everything, robbing us of ease and joy and freedom. Away with it! I am too old for it now, so I will not rationalize it in any way. As soon as I get that tense feeling, I am going straight to the Lord for deliverance. "Let us therefore come boldly unto the throne of grace, that we may obtain mercy, and find grace to help in time of need." (Heb. 4:16, KJV) I will. I am pledged to "take every thought captive" and deliver over to Christ the troublesome ones, so that his freedom and his peace may reign in me. Then my joy will break out in child dancing and wild hosannas. No excuses. It is a *choice*.

CHAPTER ELEVEN

LIGHT AFFLICTION

B ig losses and small. Large pains and small. Huge changes in
appearance and minor ones. The end of beauty, agility, and
vitality. The Bible calls this "light affliction." Old age ushers it
in, whether with significant physical pain and problems or minor ones,
and no one travels this last mile without loss and light affliction. No
matter what the compensations for these, the losses are still felt acutely
and are painful. I need to remember that this stage of life is just prior to
what the rest of the verse promises: "For our light affliction which is but
for a moment, worketh for us a far more exceeding and eternal weight of
glory." (2 Corinthians 4:17, KJV) What is this eternal weight of glory? It
is surely heaven, with all its resplendent glory, that awaits.

I find great comfort in reading 1 Corinthians 15 and thinking of the
new and glorious body that will be mine in heaven. I read Revelation
21 and 22 and revel in the description of the new Jerusalem. What

splendor. I treasure the promises of heaven and the wonders that await me there. I can hardly imagine any of this, but pictures do come to mind, and I am blessed by them even as I know that they are no doubt very inaccurate, based as they are on human experiences on earth. I meditate on these wonders as well as the wonder of ecstatic praise and life never ending that will be mine there. I think of all the people already there that I long to see and greet and fellowship with deeply and with great emotion. Above all, I long for that face to face ultimate view of God himself in all his glory. I long for his welcome; I long to behold his joy; I long to delight him with my adoration.

Since I know I will soon be departing this life, and going on to the next, I find it a valuable use of time to contemplate my future home, spending time meditating on it and less on the here and now. I do not think this is the "pie in the sky bye and bye" escape that it might be for a younger person. I am not seeking escape from life now. I am truly loosening my hold on the life on earth; this is a necessary release of the grip—a letting go of what cannot be kept for a taking hold of that which I will forever own. If I am willing to do this, I will not suffer from more than "light affliction" no matter how severe my physical ailment may be.

PART TWO

THE VALLEY OF
THE SHADOW

Even though I walk
through the valley of the shadow of
death
I will fear no evil
for you are with me
Your rod and your staff,
they comfort me.
Psalm 23:4

But he gives more grace.
James 4:6

CHAPTER TWELVE

THE NEW CRISIS

How blithely I wrote the last words of Part I. Little did I know the new valley that awaited me in the summer of 2008.

Treatment for my kidney problems had begun in December 2007. After three months, I had been overjoyed to be feeling much better. My energy level had climbed back to almost normal, though I continued to have disrupted sleep, weight gain, and other side effects from medications. Still I felt very much better, much more energetic, and almost normal. Then in April 2008, something changed—the edge was off and my energy waning. By May, I felt tired. I looked forward to summer and to being outdoors—that would lift me. But only the weather improved.

My kidney doctor adjusted my medications but my lab tests revealed no improvement. By August I felt I was back to square one, just where

I had been the previous December, except that I was thirty pounds heavier, and nothing was being done to bring down this weight. I knew it was water weight, not fat, because I had greatly increased edema, but that didn't make it easier to bear.

Back in the mire of despondency, I felt my faith weaken, my lethargy increase.

In the wee hours of the morning, unable to sleep, I cried to God, "Why? And when? When will this nightmare end?" But a change in this valley of the shadows was coming—it was growing much darker.

Just prior to August I developed a painful sore in my lower left gum just beyond my last molar. I called my dentist to have it checked, but the answer machine informed me that he and his entire staff were on summer break. As I waited for their return, the pain decreased, so my anxiety about the problem faded. I thought it just a minor infection, easily treatable.

The first day the office opened, I called and was given a slot that very afternoon. As my dentist examined me, his expression changed to one I had never seen. Usually very calm, he looked instead startled as if he were seeing something distressing. He seemed anxious as he probed, x-rayed, and took photos. Then he also used a special instrument that detects possible malignancies. He didn't report (and I didn't ask—chicken?) what he saw except to tell me I would need to see an oral surgeon as soon as possible for a biopsy. That told me all I needed to know; I had cancer! He immediately called a clinic in Nanaimo, thirty miles north, and arranged for me to see one of the oral surgeons (all three there were close colleagues of his) on the following Wednesday. Only two days wait; usually it took two months or more to see any oral surgeon. The urgency confirmed my deduction.

My sore might surely be cancerous—that was clear—yet somehow I thought its small size indicated a small problem which had been quickly detected and would likely be quickly dealt with, like a skin cancer. So I shoved down the anxious feelings and the "what if's." My kidney problems and edema were more than enough.

The oral surgeon's examination led to a speedy biopsy that Wednesday afternoon. The report arrived the following Monday—definitely cancer. That was the diagnosis I expected, but I continued in my denial of the implications. It seemed like just one more misery heaped on the energyless days, the fretful nights, the heaviness of body and mind. I was trudging through a swamp, sucked down in knee-deep mud. I felt no anger; I just longed for an end. Weariness wrapped me like a tangle of jungle vines.

The oral surgeon told me to call my family doctor and let him proceed to get me the treatment I would need. When I got the report, I called right away, only to find that he too was away on summer vacation and that I would have to wait ten days to see him. When I did, he immediately referred me to an ear, nose, and throat specialist in Duncan whom I waited several days to see. He quickly referred me to the Cancer Clinic in Victoria. Expecting a call that did not come, I called them after a few days. The lady who spoke to me assured me that I had been referred to a surgeon who specialized in my type of cancer, and that I would hear from him shortly. His office did call after a few more days, giving me an appointment for late September. More waiting. By this time several weeks had passed since the diagnosis; now anxiety pressed in. I had been assured I had a slow growing cancer, but it *was* cancer. I wondered how much it had grown and spread during all these weeks of waiting.

I saw the surgeon as scheduled. He examined the inside of my mouth and jaw extensively, probing deeply. He told me the cancer had likely taken hold of much of the left side of my mouth, cheek, and possibly my jaw bone. He said the CAT scan he would schedule for me would give verification, but he was sure it would confirm what his examination had shown him.

He then outlined my future. It was his opinion that the cancer would need to be surgically removed, and that there would be no radiation, the facial tissues being too sensitive for it. He explained that he had done hundreds of operations of the kind I would require. He said the success rate world wide on my type of cancer was 98%—that was encouraging—and that he had never experienced a failure personally. I later found out my doctor was a world renowned specialist in his field; that too was encouraging.

Just one problem—the incision would be from the outside in, a cut from the bottom of my ear, under my jaw bone, to the center of my neck, and up under my chin. The entire side of my face would be folded back to get clear access to the cancer. When all the cancer had been removed, a plastic surgeon would then take a patch from my left wrist, about three inches in length, and would replace the tissues and blood vessels that had been removed with it, reattach blood vessels, and then I would have normal function of the muscles, though some nerve damage would be lasting. A skin patch would also be taken from my upper thigh to replace the wrist patch. Bone would be removed from my leg if my jaw bone had to be removed, though this might prove unnecessary. (When later I got the results of the CAT scan, it validated everything he had told me.)

"It's brutal," he said, "but there is no other way. I later found the word "brutal" an understatement.

He further explained that I would have to have a tracheotomy and spend two weeks in the hospital. For several days I would be unable to speak or eat. After I came home I could expect the entire healing process to last six months.

I was stunned; there is no other word for it. Lynda MacDonald, a very dear friend and also a nurse, had come with me and heard it all; she joined me in my reaction. So much for a small, easily treated cancer! I think it took me days to digest the full impact of it all.

That same day he turned me over to his assistant to begin to arrange the date for surgery with Royal Jubilee Hospital in Victoria; this would require a minimum wait of two months—not his choice, but because of the line up of surgeries at the hospital. In the meantime, I was to see the plastic surgeon he referred me to, have the CAT scan, and be seen by a Cancer Clinic doctor for a second opinion. (When I did, this doctor fully concurred with the surgeon.)

Lynda and I talked and considered all that we'd heard. Later that day, back home, I talked with George. We three drew this conclusion: with my kidney problems and edema, this radical surgery was life threatening. Should I have the operation? Postpone it? Should I refuse? How long would I live if I did refuse? I'm not sure I can truly describe my state of mind at this time. In my weariness, I was somewhat resigned to my fate whatever it was. Back in the pit, I was not getting clarity when I prayed, and was again feeling immeasurably powerless, without control, old, inept, useless, and caring little whether I lived or died. Now I just longed for it all to end, one way or another.

Mustering my energy, I asked my family, especially my sister, and my friends to pray for my decision, along with George, Lynda, and my prayer partners.

After a few days of prayer and deliberation, I made my decision—I would have the operation if possible. With that I went to see the plastic surgeon I'd been referred to. His kind, gentle spirit encouraged me, and I regained a small measure of peace.

Now to wait for a surgery date. A month of silence followed. Finally the call came—the surgery date was set for November 25.

CHAPTER THIRTEEN

HOSPITAL, FIRST STAY

I am not fond of hearing all the gruesome details of an elderly person's ill-health woes. Yet here I am giving them! But I think the contrast between suffering and grace will not be evident without some detail, so at the risk of boring you I tell the following.

My edema problem became a crisis. Right after I had seen the surgeon about the cancer, I had told my kidney specialist about the pending operation. He then began taking me off the strong medications which were lowering my immune system. Leaving on his vacation, he instructed me to see my family doctor if I had any concerns while he was away. I certainly did. Soon after I stopped the medications, my edema increased alarmingly. When I sought my family doctor for help, he advised me to continue as I was and wait for my kidney specialist to return.

I found this hard to do. With the heavy water weight all through my system now, my whole body was swollen. Like a water balloon rolling about, I lumbered here and there when I had to, bought mega sized clothes at thrift stores, and had long since stopped crossing legs and cutting toe nails. Shoes were a problem—none fit my swollen feet except clogs which I wedged my feet into and house slippers with open backs. With puffed up arms and hands, I could no longer wear my watch; my rings squeezed my fingers for I couldn't get them off. Wherever I poked, I could make half inch indentations in my arms or legs. Breathing was a chore, wheezing a constant. And sleep—oh, how I longed for a full night's sleep.

Ever had a water-logged brain? I wanted to pray, read Scripture, and meditate, but I couldn't find the motivation nor the concentration. Gradually I lost hope of a future, merely managing to drag through one day at a time, merely existing. By the late days of October I realized I could not have the cancer operation in this dangerous condition. I began to feel desperate. Seeing my family doctor again, I further lost hope when he sympathized and merely ordered more tests. I took them, and waited again as instructed, but with an undercurrent of panic. I made an appointment with him again in early November. In the few days in between I gained another ten pounds. My weight was now two hundred and twelve pounds, sixty plus pounds above my normal weight. When I arrived for the appointment, my doctor took one look at me and gasped.

"Joy, what has happened to you?"

How could I answer that? I told him the facts and asked to be admitted to the hospital. Duncan didn't have the needed facilities, he said; I would need to go to Royal Jubilee in Victoria for renal care. He immediately called and talked to the doctor in charge that day, a foremost specialist who told him to have me begin greatly increased diuretics. As they talked something broke in me. It was clear—they were not going to hospitalize me; they were merely going to give me more medications! The volcano in me was erupting—the surge of anger threatened to spew out like fiery hot lava. When my doctor turned to advise me of the specialist's recommendation, I shouted,

"No, I won't! I need to go to the hospital! I need this problem to end! I will go to the Emergency in Victoria tomorrow morning!" I think the whole clinic heard me.

Though surprised by my outburst, my doctor did not try to dissuade me. Though he told me that I might not be admitted, I was more than ready to find out. He agreed that hospitalization was probably needed, but that he couldn't admit me to Royal Jubilee in Victoria. George, who had been going through much stress and anxiety about my condition, heartily concurred with my decision to try Emergency the next morning. But we both needed support. So we called our very good friends, Peter and Corinne DeLange, who had offered us help at any time. They readily agreed to take us, and did.

Early the next morning, we sat waiting for two hours in Emergency. Finally I was taken in and treatment was begun—injections of albumin to "blot up the water" and strong diuretics to flush it out, a somewhat dangerous procedure, but by now deemed a necessary risk by the resident in charge. Meanwhile George and our friends waited, walked about, went to eat, waited some more, came in to see me from time to time (angels!), until at last at eight that evening, the admitting kidney doctor finally arrived. He took one look at me and immediately admitted me to the renal wing. He assured us that I would be there several days.

I spent eight days in the hospital, November 8 through 16. I continued to receive the same treatment that had been given me in Emergency, with the same results: my weight dropped dramatically. The relief I felt was immense, growing daily. My gratitude to God matched it, and my sense of his presence and love returned as I laughed joyously with the friends who visited. Now I could hear the woes of my roommate and share Christ with him.

In those eight days, I lost over forty-five pounds. My loss was the talk of the entire wing—I could hear the buzz about it in the halls. My kidney specialist returned later that week, very attentive and concerned. The eighth day I was told I could go home, that more treatment would not be advisable. Enough. Time to celebrate!

Though my strength and energy were still low since my kidney problems were still present, I was overjoyed to be home, to be with George, to shower and wash my hair, to stuff myself with favorite foods, to sleep in our big comfortable bed, and especially to be near my normal size again. I gleefully cast aside my oversized bag woman wear, stuffing it in plastic bags to be donated back to the thrift store as soon as possible. I was overjoyed too that I had 'kept my former clothes I'd grown too large to wear for almost a year. When someone had asked me why, I had replied, "It's my hope chest." Now I opened that chest. Out came a whole new wardrobe (yes, more than a year or far older, to be sure, but new almost, and new to the new me!). Hope sprang up, a fountain in me!

Now I looked ahead to the surgery date, the twenty-fifth, only a few days away. Perhaps the joy of being rid of the edema, or the joy of feeling almost normal again, kept me from apprehension; I now felt instead an assurance that I was going to live through the surgery. "Through" was the operative word. "Yea, though I walk through the valley of the shadow of death . . . " In my spirit I sensed God assuring me, "*WE* are going *THROUGH*." Peace enveloped me.

CHAPTER FOUTEEN

HOSPITAL, SECOND STAY

The last few days at home I spent preparing for the surgery. I made a sustained effort to request prayer— from family, church, friends near and far; indeed from everyone I could think of. And what responses I recieved! Words of comfort, care, and assurances, of promises of continuing prayer, of teams of people being formed to pray. Several churches put me on their prayer lists, in Texas, in California, in Oregon, and in British Columbia. I felt wrapped in a warm blanket of love.

Why so much prayer? Why so many enlisted to pray? I asked for prayer without requesting that I be healed or made well. I gave the facts about my condition and pending surgery and then wrote, "Pray as you are led by the Spirit." I did make one request: that my faith be sustained. I consider any prayer an opportunity to connect with God, to trust him, to fellowship with him. Thus I truly believed my request for prayer offered potential blessing to each one who responded. I do not fully comprehend the workings and wonder of prayer, but I do believe, both from Scripture and from my experience, that prayer opens the channel for the love of God to flow to the one who prays as well as to the one prayed for—a double blessing.

I too returned to the joy of continuing prayer and dialogue with the Lord in those few days awaiting surgery. I confessed and repented of my earlier despair and distancing, and now believed I would trust God fully in his choice for me, whether life or death. Even though I felt much better now that my edema problems had been dealt with, I knew what I was facing, or thought I did. Yet I now knew an immense peace and a sense of well-being, and a flow of gratitude. "It is well with my soul."

George and I drove to Victoria the afternoon before my surgery, booked into a near-by motel, and had a last slow and satisfying meal, full of succulent beef. I showered with special soap as directed, and then we went to bed early, anticipating our early rising. We had been told to be at the hospital at 6 A.M. As I drifted toward sleep, I wondered if this would be my last night on earth, though I registered no fear. Again I sensed a strong assurance that "*WE* are going *THROUGH.*"

> Yea, though I walk through the valley of the shadow of death,
> I will fear no evil; for *Thou* art with me . . . "
>
> (Psalm 23:4. KJV, emphasis mine)

November 25, 2008. 7:30 A.M. All the registering, the gowning, and the pre-op prep work had been done. George gave me a last quick hug and kiss as an attendant wheeled me away. The short ride through busy corridors gave me only time to grasp God's hand and commit all to him. In the operating theatre, my anesthesiologist greeted me, applied his skill, and that was all I knew. Such utter "outness" is hard to comprehend. I was later told that the operation lasted over five hours.

No glitches, no surprises. All went well and according to plan, I was told.

I had not been dreaming when I regained consciousness, but I awoke to a nightmare. It began late that afternoon; I had no sense of the passage of time but full awareness of immense changes in me. I could hardly believe the state I was in. My face felt incredibly swollen, the left side totally numb, my tongue in pain, huge and protruding from my mouth, my lips cracked, painful, and incredibly dry, my breathing labored, and my lungs congested. The tracheotomy tube (how strange and strangling it felt), the nose tube, the IV, the patches, everything seemed foreign to me, constricting. For the next three days I would wish fervently from time to time that I had never awakened. I was not in great pain. Repeated injections of morphine took care of that. But if there is a misery beyond pain, I was in it.

Not allowed to drink, I was tortured by my thirst. I was fed and given medicines by the tube in my nose which was often snagged, causing intense pain.

The large tracheotomy tube clogged up often so that breathing became an effort. Fear would grip me as I labored to suck in air. My lungs were infected and very congested so that I coughed frequently, wheezed and struggled. This brought on a nurse who would then insert a probe in the breathing pathway of my trach, then push it up and down to make me cough more. This procedure would bring up the infected matter; the nurse would then remove an insert in the trach, clear the passageway, and reinsert it so I could breathe again. This whole sequence was pure agony for me.

I was alternately burning hot or so cold that I shook violently. I begged for cover; I threw off cover.

I would drift into sleep, only to awake after what I hoped had been an hour or more, only to find that a single minute or two had passed.

So many tubes and wires were running in and out of me that I felt like Gulliver strapped down by the Lilliputians. More than that, my right hand and arm were a human pin-cushion. For some reason the IV in my right arm keep slipping out and having to be replaced, requiring a very hurtful probing with a large needle and a jabbing to make it stick. My left arm had the surgical patch, and I was told to keep it still and elevated; no needles were allowed in it. But my right arm, which held the IV, was also used for blood tests taken frequently, and my right fingers pricked to test blood sugar. Needles in, needles out, prick, pierce, probe for a vein somewhere that would still give blood.

Though I was able to sit up if aided, I was too weak to want to. So I lay, face up, longing for a comfortable position. I had frequent muscle spasms and cramps and writhed in agony.

I could not speak. I wrote what I had to communicate on a small board, barely able to hold the marker. I resorted to sign language whenever I could make myself understood— always my first option.

These first three days following surgery were the longest of my life. I was so utterly miserable that from time to time I did beg God, as I thought never to do, to end it.

"I know others have borne much worse pain. But I can't take this. No more, I beg. Let me go. Please let me go!"

I lived on. As my anger and frustration mounted, I charged God with lack of love. Then I challenged him, "If I am to live, give me grace! Give me something that will enable me to bear this!"

And he did. I called them "grace notes," like notes of beautiful music.

CHAPTER FIFTEEN

GRACE NOTES

The first grace note blessed me beyond measure. It was day one after my surgery. My parched throat, my hugely swollen tongue, my swollen, cracked, and very dry lips all begged for moisture. How I yearned for what I could not have—water. I knew I could not drink, and that any request for water would be denied. But then a nurse, young and beautiful, she of the soft brown angel eyes, came with an amazing thing—a narrow four inch bottle of water that had a spray top. She sprayed my lips with it! Bliss!

Did my eyes thank her? I "signed" it and a request: could I have the bottle left on my tray? She smiled, eyes lit with compassion, and left it near so I could reach it. As soon as she left, I groped for it, snatched it and held it to my breast like a mother with a newborn. Then oh, how I sprayed! Again and again. Oh the bliss of spraying not only my lips, but into my mouth, of feeling the wetness on my tongue, of "drinking" a few drops, of bathing my hot face. The oasis well in a hot desert. Such grace! Pure *hesed*.

But invariably, after a moment or two of bliss, I would sink back into inevitable misery. A new woe was added when I got a first view of my face. It was as it felt, in a word, grotesque: swollen hugely on the left side, lop-sided, my bottom lip drawn strongly down and to the right side. On seeing it, despair and anger suffused me. This was more than brutal; this was devastating. "Why, God? Why? Why must I endure this? What a monstrosity!" I heard no answer. Did the clamor inside prevent it?

My misery increased. My lung condition grew worse, my congestion acute. My night nurse was particularly quick, when I coughed, to reach for the trach probe, to ram it fiercely up and down until I coughed relentlessly. Unable to speak, I couldn't voice my reaction, but signed again and again that she should stop. She didn't.

The next day she approached me again, ready to begin her probe. I shook my head as vigorously as I could.

"If I don't do this, your pneumonia will get worse and then you will be in serious trouble," she warned. How forceful and righteous she sounded, an Old Testament prophet with dire tidings and bold pronouncements. She moved toward me, holding the probe like a weapon of attack. I cringed. Then I surprised myself and her as well with my strength—I grabbed her arm and shoved it away.

Surprised but clearly frustrated, she paused. "I *have* to do this," she insisted. I grabbed my board and wrote, "I'd rather die." I meant it. She was stunned. Obviously this broke new ground in her experience. Unsure, confused, and wounded, she simply retreated. I felt neither remorse nor triumph, just relief.

The following evening she appeared again. At the sight of her, I tensed. I felt sudden anger and prepared myself for renewed resistance.

"I came to apologize," she said. "I ought to have been more gentle. I'm sorry."

I nodded and wrote "Thank you" on my board. "What grace!" I thought, "or mercy!" Then I thought of the nurses who gave me care. Each tended me like a mother's child; eyes, arms, hands, and voices gentle, filled with care. I eagerly drank their waters of kindness. Beautiful grace notes.

CHAPTER SIXTEEN

OCEANS

Still the time inched by, ever so slowly. Each day seemed endless; nights too, for sleep came no more easily then than in the day. My discomfort continued; my misery abated for only short moments. My tiredness was bone deep; my weakness turned my bones to jelly. With the limited use of my right hand, I tried to hold a book, but found I had a one minute limit. But then it didn't matter much—I simply could not concentrate, even on the lightest subject matter, nor could I pray except to plead for help. My dialogue with God ceased; intercession—usually a joy—seemed impossible. Without radio, music, or TV, there was no distraction from my land of misery.

My room's decor featured medical essentials, trays and bowls, bottles and tubes; no pictures or wall hangings competed with the few warning posters. Out the windows on my left, I could view the other wing of the mustard brown building and little else. I could see one thing clearly—the weather; it held true to late November, rainy, cold and gray. I could not converse with my roommate, obviously deep in her own agony if sounds told her story, even if either of us had felt up to it, which we didn't. Lacking an outward focus, I found myself left to acute awareness of my miserable, sweating, freezing, aching, suffocating, itching, hurting self.

"Oh God, I am no victor. I hate this! I can't bear it one more minute! Let me go! Please let me go!" I lived on.

"Then give me more grace to bear it!" And he did. The second day I received an assignment. By that I mean I sensed God answering my plea. In my mind I sensed a clear instruction: "Revisit every ocean you have been in or on." The prospect immediately excited me. A quick re-cap video flashed scene after scene. Yes, I would slowly visit each one, recalling every sensual perception I had had, reveling in sight and sound, in touch and taste and smell, savoring each as fully as I could. I would retreat into this land of memory and vivid imagination.

I decided to move chronologically in order not to miss any experience. So I began with the only time I experienced the ocean (actually the Gulf of Mexico) as a child. I was very young, not more than three or four. I was with my parents, brother, aunt, uncle, and cousins at Galveston. When my dad put me down in the water, the low surf surged against me, tugging at me, dragging me out. I screamed in terror and begged to be rescued. Somehow it didn't traumatize me. When I next experienced the ocean, I became a life-long convert.

In my late twenties, I was hired as head counselor of a girls' camp in Maine for the summer. I was studying for a master's degree at Baylor University in Waco, Texas, so I invited a friend I'd met there, Sherry, to come with me to work at the camp. Together we planned a seventeen day trip by car, a slow exploration up the east coast and inland mountains as we went, moving and stopping as it struck our fancy. We started out in my old Dodge from home in Texas, made our way across the deep South, bijou country, and meandered up the Atlantic Coast, occasionally catching sight of the vast Atlantic and the stretches of marsh, sand, and sea grass along the Carolinas. For some reason we didn't stop to explore the ocean itself, knowing we'd be near it all summer. Instead we headed into the mountains.

When we reached New York City, we spent several days sight-seeing (now there's a story!) Then after much of that amazing city, we decided to visit Jones Beach, breathe in the open air, stretch out in the sun, and experience the vast Atlantic first hand. There I gazed in amazement at the endless ocean, then joyfully plunged in, exulting in the steep waves that rolled to shore, finding myself tossed and whirled and scraped on the bottom as I rode them in. Not like pools in Texas, warm as bath water. But I loved it!

We spent a few more days sightseeing as we headed north, then came to the enchantment of Cape Cod. Scenic sea sides, rolling waves, picturesque towns, cottages, all picture pretty. Looking was not enough. We slid down the sand cliffs for hours and dreamed by that gentle surf, our thoughts breeding wistful poetry.

In Maine before camp commenced, we two visited the nearest beach. The June day was unseasonably hot, and perfect for play. The stretches of sand lay broad and warm, inviting sun bathing. Emboldened by the heat, we made daring rushes into the icy waters, screaming with joyous agony, and plunging about madly for brief moments before running to our towels, grabbing them up to swath our shivering bodies like rejuvenating mummies, and then slowly unwrapping to lie blissfully in the sun until we took courage to do it all again. In my mind, in my sickbed, I relived it all, loving, laughing, longing. How fresh it seemed.

Other times that summer I remember walking along rocky paths at the oceanside, and sitting mesmerized as I watched tons of water launch themselves against those massive rock cliffs, bursting into white tossed spray, glittering bright in the sunlight, piercing my heart with their powerful beauty. How small I felt, lonely and full of longings.

Once or twice with male counselors from the near-by boys' camp, we went to coves to feast on clams and lobster. The foggy air, the strong odor of fish and gear and lines, the gummy wet clams, their amazing shells, the cracking and retrieving the tasty morsels—all came back to me with vividness and great pleasure.

The following year I moved to Maryland for a teaching position. I remembered being invited to go sailing on the Chesapeake Bay. Here I had yet another taste of the Atlantic shore. Sweet intoxication—to ride the waves, through bright seas below a vivid blue sky, the boat cleaving the waters at that slanted angle that fills sails and heaves up spray. I clutched the side, drunk with the roll and exhilaration of it all. The best of wines.

One spring break a fellow teacher and I decided to travel to Florida. We drove down the Atlantic coast to West Palm Beach, where the sun shone bright and clear, making the warm ocean waters perfect for lingering. How gladly I remembered long stretches of bouncing in the waves, riding them to shore, floating, swimming, diving in, under, and over—a child at play, uninhibited and free.

In the years that followed I married and moved to California. I renounced my first love, the Atlantic, and began my love affair with the Pacific. I never found the fifty-five degrees water warm enough for long hours of swimming, but with youth, vigor, and daring, I always dived in. It was the only way I could get in; I could never do it slowly. While living in Anaheim, we took weekly trips to Laguna Beach in the summer. There I played and laughed and flailed about with my step-children, Kenron, then about six, and Karen, eight, splashing and boogie boarding and riding our small water raft, always waiting for that perfect wave to ride to shore, then lying wet and winded in the sun.

Sometimes I swam the raft beyond the breakers, then climbed in to sun and float, gently rocked by the smooth surge of building waves. Day's end was always too soon.

This lasted about three years. Then my son Glen was born and shortly afterwards we moved to the beautiful Santa Inez Valley, about thirty-five miles north of Santa Barbara, just over the coastal mountains. Now we were much closer to three beaches, each having its own attractions. Gaviota, closest at eleven miles, was great for day-tripping. Waves rounded the rocky cliffs and rolled into shore, inviting the surf board riders as well as those of us who rode our lowly boogie boards. A few miles south lay Refugio, a half-mooned bay spread with a carpet of green grass, and beyond long stretches of palm trees and sand, great for waves that rounded the corner of the cliffs to the north. The variety of beauty drew me to long and meditative walks. A third beach lay a few more miles further south, the sprawling El Capitan, with its excellent extensive campsites nestled among live oaks, except for the new division which lay on grass along the hill, offering great walkways for star-gazers. There were miles of trails to explore and beaches to play on.

Glen took after his siblings: he was totally unafraid of water. He resisted the lessons at the local pool, preferring to teach himself to swim, and was fearless by six. It was pure joy to take my three children to the beach. I played as hard as they did. We went frequently to these beaches until the two older ones, now teenagers, opted to go with friends rather than Mom.

Sherry, the friend with whom I had traveled to Maine, was now married, had two children near Glen's age, and lived in San Diego. We agreed to meet for a week long camp-out at El Capitan with our three young ones. We knew we would not have to think up ways to entertain these ocean loving children. They played without giving us a moment's fret for hours, splashing, riding the waves, building sand castles, and exploring sea life. That freed us to play in the water too, or to talk, reminisce, gaze at the waves to our hearts' content, or lie silent, soaking up peace and sunshine. Our only problem was getting the kids to come out of the water. Hunger did it. In the long evenings we grilled our hot dogs over open fire pits, roasted marshmallows, told stories, and then went star-gazing. On the top of the hill we looked down on the ocean, the moon making a silver path on the shimmering water. On warm nights we strolled the shore, toes digging into wet sand, water lapping at our ankles, as we watch each slow wave, tipped by silver, roll in at angles, wave after wave, as far as the eye could see.

In my hospital bed I was transported, slowly living it all again, focused beyond myself into the indescribable beauty, peace, and goodness of it all.

I also recalled trips north along the coast during these years, sometimes with family, sometimes with friends, to Pismo, Morrow Bay, Cambria, and San Simeon. I lingered in my memories of each. I particularly remembered walking alone along the shore in Cambria and hearing the sound of a bagpipe. I searched for it. There about a half mile away stood a man on a rock, playing the plaintive and winsome "Amazing Grace," each note clear and poignant in that ocean setting.

How indelible is my memory of the incredible cliffs of the Big Sur. I visited this majestic stretch of coastline several times. There I peered again and again from those rocky cliffs to an endless ocean, so vast and untamed. Once Glen, now a young man, and I hiked into a campsite right at cliff's edge, loving the inlet, the turquoise waters, the waterfalls, the cliff edges with the waves crashing in and through the rock formations, and that evening in the twilight—how splendid— otters swimming lazily in the waves below. We drove over magnificent bridges, the mountains rising steeply to the right, the ocean far below us and to the left. Such vast beauty! In my hospital bed I lingered in the memory.

Other trips came to mind: San Francisco and the Golden Gate, Monterrey Bay and Carmel with its white sands, the coasts of northern California and Oregon, coasts often shrouded with fog and mist and memory making. Also Europe: I crossed the English Channel at Dover, its white cliffs echoing memories of Word War II, in a hover craft, speeding to France. I traveled to Hawaii and swam in Maui's warm coastal waters. I snorkled there, meeting small beautifully colored fish face to face, marveling afresh at the variety of God's handiwork.

Some of these trips had been after my move, alone, to Santa Barbara in my fifties. Personal devastation and depression had pulled me into doubts and questions, very weakened faith, and wandering far from God into psychological theory, Jungian thinking, New Age fantasies, and disastrous relationships. In desperation, I returned in great sorrow, repentance, and renewed surrender to God. In a new place of humility and trembling, I stayed very close to him, finding great joy in his fellowship. It was there along the beautiful shores of the Santa Barbara Channel that I learned lament and fresh beginnings until union with Christ became the chief focus of my life. Sunday afternoons often found me walking along one of the many beautiful beaches. Here's one:

Sunday

Boats nestle on the gray-blue breast;
Pelicans sweep the feather-dippled water;
Near shore the surf song murmurs
And ends in milky sibilance.

Sandpipers call and probe,
Then perch on one leg, stick stilts,
Awaiting another lisping wave.

Sun and clouds play hide and seek,
Spreading ribbons on sky and sea,
Peach-gold and pewter.

Three boys in short wetsuits
Wait on a towering rock
For a wild wave to thrash itself.
One launches, butt first, into the sprung spray
And washes in with pride.

I stride along a wet sand shelf.
And coax the sun to spread silver at my side.
The sea breeze sweeps my soul clean.

To my right the mountains rise
And stretch beyond in variegated blues
Of rock ribbed land and sky and bend
Beckoning me to tomorrow.

Not yet. It's Sunday.
My loosened mind, reflective soul, my spirit
Crave companioning with Christ,
His pace, His place.

Now the coast lay close at hand and I walked it almost daily, never
tiring of watching the waves roll in, or gazing out from cliffs above,
or seeking to see the beautiful life that lay in the tide pools. The years
following were times of deepest abiding. How his presence and his love
renewed and sustained me day by day. It was there I learned to be utterly
transparent with him, to hide nothing, to play no games, to refuse to
be "religious", and to stop striving. Ocean walks with my best friend,
my Lord Jesus, were a necessity, giving ultimate satisfaction, peace, and
deepening joy. I still played in the water now and then, but now my
inner life had grown larger than my outer. I relished these times with my
great God, strolling along the vast ocean he had created.

Once I took a trip on a small boat holding about thirty passengers to one of the Channel Islands. On the way over we spotted dolphins, leaping and playing, some riding the wake right beside the boat. Suddenly they were all around us, everywhere we looked, thrusting themselves out of the water, splashing in again in graceful arcs, darting and cavorting. Surely we were seeing at least five hundred of them, performing their best for us. How incredible it seemed, yet there they were, seeming as excited as we were, having a party with us!

A last ocean memory from years in California came back to me—my long awaited trip to Alaska. I had looked for three years to find just the combination of sea/land tour that I wanted. At last I found it and booked it. I was now sixty-four and growing a bit tired. I kept feeling the nudge to retire from my counseling profession, although I had previously planned to work for several more years. But where to go and what to do I hadn't a clue. Meanwhile I would take my dream trip to Alaska. So I did. That's when I viewed the magnificent Inland Passage for the first time.

And that's where I met George Brewster, a widower from Duncan, British Columbia, whom I would later marry (how utterly astounding to us both!). And now for the past eleven years I have loved the beautiful bays of Vancouver Island where I have been blessed to live. With George I have also seen the wonders of the south Pacific around New Zealand, traveled the Mediterranean, the Caribbean, the coast of Colombia, the Panama Canal, the Florida Keys, the Cape Breton coast, ever fascinated by the many faces of the oceans. In my hospital bed, I lingered again over each.

What grace I had experienced as I completed this assignment. My heart was filled with gratitude. Lest I return to too great an awareness of myself, I hastened to pray, "What next, Lord? Please give me another assignment."

CHAPTER SEVENTEEN

MOUNTAINS

Mountains. The word came quickly to my mind—my second assignment on the grace road. I was excited, ready to begin, and did. Though my memory times were frequently interrupted with checks of vital signs, trach, and operation sites, many blood tests, IV's, tube feedings and medications, I steadfastly returned from each to my memory excursions. Each return seemed a new "grace" to me.

Mountain memories were an even greater delight than my ocean visits. Each one I entered into and lived again to the fullest extent possible, beginning with the Colorado Rockies when I was a junior in high school on a glorious trip planned and executed by our Young Life leader. I truly fell in love with mountains from my first sight of them. I had seen nothing like them in our prairie flatland in Texas. Their magnificence, their grandeur, their vastness, their colors and formations—everything about them fascinated me! My first view of them burned in my memory and the awe accompanying it.

Somewhere along the way I made it my goal to climb every mountain range in America. My knees gave out in my sixties, so I didn't quite make it. But I think I did see them all and did hike in many. After the Rockies, I hiked in the Presidential Range in New England, the Appalachians—the Blue Ridge, the Great Smoky Mountains, and the Ozarks before moving west. In my hospital room I revisited each, savoring the effortful climbs, the redolence and view of evergreens and herbs, the many and varied mountain wildflowers, the pure flowing streams and waterfalls, the magnificent views from craggy outcroppings and peaks—all the beauty of God's design, large and small. I was utterly delighted, breathing afresh the exhilarating air, gazing at the deep blue of the sky, smelling the fresh green of trees and grasses, feeling the sweat of my effort and the grand gladness of each rest, and sharing all this, and sighs and laughter with fellow climbers. Mountain hiking became my favorite outdoor adventure; I never exhausted my longing to see what was around the next bend, over the next rise, up to the next great viewpoint.

In the west, I saw again, as I had the first time, the immense spaces in the high plateau country of New Mexico and Arizona, with their towering pinnacle rocks and ridges. Then California—what an abundance of mountains there. On a trip into the Sierra Nevada, I saw incredible Yosemite for the first time from the top of the Tioga Pass. Tears burst forth from an overfull heart as I gazed, consumed by awe and wonder. When I stood in the spray of Yosemite Falls looking up, I was again caught up in amazement, my tears flowing and unstoppable. Oh what a God of wonder who created such incredible magnificence and beauty!

I continued to hike as often as I could: I climbed Mount San Jacinto and other mountains east of Los Angeles, I struggled a good distance up Mount Whitney, and I hiked and climbed in several National Parks, especially King's Canyon and Sequoia. When we moved from Anaheim to the Santa Inez Valley, I was overjoyed to find mountains surrounding me. In the years that followed, I hiked and explored them again and again, ever delighted with my outings.

One trip I took was a strenuous one which I planned with three other "girls." I was then in my forties; they were all a bit younger. We prepared diligently, practicing with forty pound backpacks. Our day arrived: in great excitement we began in the giant Sequoias and made our way along back trails, savoring the moments. But one of us became a drag—*me*—I developed altitude sickness. So we slowed down, set up camp, slept under the vast sky, and sure enough, I was acclimated and fine in the morning. Same scenario the next day, same result. Finally on our fourth day, we set ourselves to reach our goal. They moved out ahead, thinking I wouldn't attempt it. But I did—with mincing steps and s-l-o-w, I finally joined them at ten thousand plus feet, queen of all I surveyed. What triumph!

In Switzerland I rode a gondola up another ten thousand plus peak to walk through blue ice caves in the glacier, and then to view the towering stretch of snow-covered Alps, an endless expanse, and to gaze down, down, down through intermittent clouds to the green pastures below and the tiny dots of cattle.

The sharp pinnacles of the Tetons in Wyoming, the wonders of Yellowstone, and the rising shires of the Olympics gave me great delight. Through the years I saw the Cascades many times, each with its own magnificence. Of course, now living in Duncan, I had only to look out from the east coast of Vancouver Island as I drove north to see the snow covered coastal mountains of British Columbia right across the channel.

Right where I now live, just as in Santa Inez and Santa Barbara, I am blessed to look out at the surrounding mountains every day, though Californians would call them hills.

My first tour of the Canadian Rockies, so clear in my mind, was a surprise. I had seen mountains before, many of them, but there is something magical about the magnificence and beauty of these northern Rockies. On the tour my face was glued to the coach window, unwilling to miss a single sight. At our first stop I hurried from the coach to get out and to view these mountains unhindered, to feel the sharp, cold air, to breathe it, to whirl around, taking in every scene, to shout with joy. Over the years George and I have traveled to them and through them many times, each time to be freshly amazed at unsurpassed beauty and to praise the Creator again.

From my hospital bed I visited these many mountains, amazed at the fullness of my memory and filled with thankfulness and gratitude to God. I felt his presence with me, his delight in my delight as we recalled his handiwork together.

Most magnificent of all I've ever viewed is Denali, formerly called Mount McKinley. At 23,320 feet, it is the loftiest mountain in North America. On my trip to Alaska, I said good-bye to my new friend George at Skagway, took the wonderfully fun trip through rugged coastal mountains on the splendid narrow-gage railway to White Horse in the Yukon (built for the gold-rushers), then flew back to Anchorage for a two day visit before heading by train to Denali Park. How I hoped that morning as I boarded that the rain would clear, the clouds disappear, and Denali could be seen. But it seemed not to be, for the rain and fog and drizzle persisted, and seem to grow greater if anything during the eight hour ride. I resigned myself. "Maybe tomorrow," I told myself, knowing I had another day before we returned to Anchorage.

Just as we arrived at five P.M., the sun broke through, the clouds fled away, and there stood before me magnificent mountains, and beyond them, Denali! I ran into the lodge nearby where tickets were being sold for flight viewing.

"Are there any flight viewings for Denali today?" I gasped.

The pretty attendant was unperturbed. "The last one is about to leave. I have one more space available."

"I'll take it," I was almost yelling in my excitement.

She handed me the ticket, took my money, and pointed me to a near-by room. "You'll need to hurry. They are preparing to board right now."

I dashed into the room and let it be known that I was the final passenger. Was it because I was last that I was given the very best seat, right next to the pilot? Amazing! I could hardly believe this was happening. I hauled out the cheap throw away camera my brother-in-law had advised me to buy. I was no camera buff and rarely took pictures of any kind, but he had assured me I couldn't miss finding something I'd want to shoot, and if it didn't turn out well, I wouldn't have much invested. (This was prior to the digital.) Well, I thought, even if I get a fuzzy one, as I usually do, it will be fun to try.

The pilot had had many years of experience. We passengers felt it in his confidence as the plane lifted off and he began to talk of the magnificent mountains before us. He spun out his tale of the history of Denali as we made our way toward the giant. We soared over the lesser mountains until we flew directly toward it, an unbelievably big mountain in the distance, fully in view in all its splendor, snow covered and impossibly majestic. It grew larger and larger as I grew more and more amazed, completely awed by the sheer size and grandeur, pristine and clear in its mantel of white against a deep blue sky. Finally we reached the mountain itself. Below us now on the mountainside we spotted a cluster of tents, each looking like a ladybug on a tilted white sheet, and some of the hikers, mere dots on the landscape. On we flew straight towards the peak, then climbed to view it at the top. To look down from that lofty height—what an unforgettable experience, a sense of soaring like an eagle.

The pilot explained that he would do a fly-by and that he would tell us the exact moment to snap our pictures. I had the advantage of the wide window on my right. I waited breathlessly and then snapped the moment the signal came. I took the picture of a lifetime! It was perfect and complete, clear and utterly amazing. I felt totally jubilant when I saw it.

But on that extraordinary afternoon I was seeing the real thing, and I found it beyond me to fully assimilate all I was seeing, for I saw the entire mountain top to bottom.

"So big, so big," I thought. An inner voice answered, "And I am bigger still." At that moment I envisioned Christ standing in front of Denali, larger, grander, more magnificent, the utterly strong, the unutterably Great. Lord of all. My Jesus.

It was sheer joy to me to relive that adventure. How vivid it was to me as I lay, transported by the gift of memory.

My entire revisit to the mountains of my life was grace upon grace. For as much as I loved oceans, I loved mountains even more. I felt showered with the blessing of it all, and filled with gratitude, wonder, and peace. I didn't want it to end and played it out as long as I could. I thanked God for the assignment, and of course I would have asked for more had not a new grace note arrived.

CHAPTER EIGHTEEN

MUSIC

Before I asked for another assignment, I received a new grace note, unasked for and unexpected. Corinne, Peter, and George came to visit. Corinne gave me a small CD player with earphones and an album of Christmas music. George brought a CD of old hymns. Music! Who can account for the blessing it brings? I listened to the Christmas music eagerly, soaking in it. Yet, having heard it, I hit an emotional snag, thinking of all I was missing of the Christmas season as I lay in my bed of misery. How quickly the wonder of the former grace notes faded. How brief my gratitude. How heavily the present weighed in. Again I began to feel angry and wronged by the entire awfulness of present reality. Thinking of my weakened body and disfigured face, I began again to hear in myself the angry doubts, and to berate God, "If you loved me, why would you allow this? Yes, you have given me many blessings, but this is cruel and brutal. Is this love? Why does this have to happen to me?" How quickly I slipped into this pit of self-pity.

Finally, needing distraction again, I slipped the hymn disc into the CD player. I had known the words to these hymns since my early childhood, but I refused to sing along, my thinking instead lingering on caustic and critical accusations. I remember thinking, "Yes, yes, I know you say you love me. I just find it hard to believe." You may find my ungrateful attitude hard to understand after the ways the assignments had blessed me. I find it hard to understand myself now. I do know it was very easy to become aware again of the misery of my present, and in my weakened state of mind, to become negative and despairing.

At that moment another song came on. I do not know which one, nor do I remember the words being sung, though I may have known them well. But as it was sung, I heard the Lord's voice in my mind:

"Yes, but *you love me*!"

I was totally astonished at these words, and at that moment I envisioned him looking at me with incredible wistfulness and yearning. He didn't say, "I love you." He said, "you love me"! Something broke in me and I began to weep, then to sob, as an enormous realization swept over me.

"Yes, yes, I do. I do. I love you. I have loved you so long! Now I can't live without that love," I thought. Then, without these exact words but with clear understanding, I thought, "No matter what I endure, I cannot live without our relationship. The meaning of my being is found in our union. It is Life beyond life. Oh I see! I love you! I do love you."

At last I understood fully: His lovingkindness is better than life. This was ultimate grace, the glorious awareness of the preciousness of this Companion of my heart, my dearest love, my glorious Savior, my incredible God. I wept and wept with the wonder of it.

No ocean, no mountain, no person—even the dearest— no experience of any kind can begin to compare with the profound fulfillment, the unutterable joy, the indescribable richness of my oneness with Christ, of the love relationship that is ours.

From that time on in the hospital, a new dimension of his presence was mine and though self-pity reasserted itself from time to time, I was quick to release it and to re-embrace our love, and to go on *through*.

CHAPTER NINETEEN

WATER

Two more grace notes came in those remaining days of my stay. The first of the two had again to do with water. After a few days in the hospital, I was assured that the large trach would be exchanged for a smaller one, and that I would then be able to drink and to eat a few liquid foods. I was also assured I would be able to talk. I looked forward to this fervently, especially being able to drink. My spray bottle had helped, but oh how I yearned to have an honest drink of water. It was the one tangible thing I desired most.

I could do without the talking, since I couldn't. Also, by this time I had developed a case of shingles (more Poor Me! I itched!). Since it was considered contagious, my suitemate was promptly moved out. All medical personnel and visitors had to don protective coats and gloves. I felt like a nuisance, an unwanted child. Certainly the doctor who discovered it voiced his exasperation in no uncertain terms (unrepeatable).

I was more alone than ever. But the Lord was there; his presence brought me a comfort beyond expression. In truth I never felt alone. Nothing could be done about the shingles except for medication, and mercifully it helped greatly. But water—oh, how I longed for water!

One night I even dreamed of water, of long cold cups of it, quenching my thirst, pouring in streams and abundance on my face, down my chest, ending the dryness inside and out.

Every day my surgeon appeared to check my progress, and he was pleased. Yet he debated when to remove the large trach, deciding again and again to "give it another day." The very next morning after my dream, my surgeon appeared as usual, took a quick look at my mouth, and deftly removed my trach with hardly a word. I had no time to be afraid and felt little pain. Just as quickly, he inserted the new smaller one.

"Now, how's that?" he asked, and explained that if I held my finger over it, I could talk.

I did as instructed, fumbled a bit, and tried again. "Fine," I croaked. Next breath, "Could I have a glass of water?"

He turned abruptly. "Nurse, give Mrs. Brewster a glass of water." And with that he strode away. (What did he think I'd say? I think he may have been expecting some praise I didn't give, focused as I was on my great desire. But I knew whom to praise.)

"Oh God, thank you!" I voiced inwardly, smiling my delight. The moment had come! The nurse handed me a full glass of cold water, ice included. I grasped it like a miner reaching for gold. I drank half straight down as quickly as I could, which actually was quite slowly. It was difficult for me to swallow with the small trach there and with swollen tissues, but I managed. I drank and drank and drank, slowly but joyfully, finally pausing only to breathe. Oh the sheer bliss of it! At that moment I recalled drinking water from a mountain waterfall, the extravagant bounty and purity of it overflowing my cup. I drank the rest of that glassful and later two more, each with enormous relish and pure pleasure. I shall not die but live!

"As the deer pants for the water brooks/ So my soul pants for Thee, O God." These words rose in me. I realized afresh how greatly I had thirsted for Jesus himself, the true water of Life. To the Samaritan woman at the well, he had said he would give living water. What fresh new understanding of that I now had, for she was dying of spiritual thirst, a thirst greater than mine for actual water. And later at the feast, he cried to the crowd, "If anyone is thirsty, let him come to me and drink. Whoever believes in me, as the Scripture has said, streams of living water will flow from within him." (John 7:37) Water. As he, the water of Life flows in, we well up and overflow, as springs, giving out this water to all who would drink. Again I realized with great clarity that *nothing* but the abundant flow of Christ's love would satisfy my thirsty soul. But drinking in Jesus' love is not like drinking a glass of water; it is like sitting under a waterfall!

And so I lived on, at peace now with his decision to bring me through. My days grew easier as I healed and became more mobile and used my slurry voice, laughed with visitors, relished companioning, listened to music, and joked with my nurses and attendants. Now I could read the Psalms, sing songs, feel gratitude, enjoy the Scriptures, all in his fellowship.

CHAPTER TWENTY

RELATIONSHIPS

During my last week in the hospital, I received a new assignment: "review your life relationships." I had not expected it, since I was doing and looking much better and not in the misery I had formerly been in a few days before. I did have lots of time left, though, each day of which I now spent reading and thinking and hearing music and praying and interceding. Clearly though I had received a new assignment. I both welcomed it and drew back from it—there had been so many both good and bad relationships in my life. But I committed myself to obey, asking for the Spirit's enablement to be transparent and thorough and utterly truthful.

In my usual chronological fashion I began with my earliest memories and proceeded through the years. In spite of the many interruptions that were part of my hospital day, I persisted. It took me days. Bring back to memory all the relationships of your life, beginning with parents—

amazing how many there are, isn't it? I had three great realizations in the process.

Though I wanted to, I did not hedge; I recalled the loving relationships, certainly, but also the hurts, trials, rejections, crises, and devastations. Deep memories arose of immense emotional pain I suffered during many long stretches in my life. In regard to these, I had long ago invited Jesus to be my Wonderful Counselor and my Great Physician, and indeed he had been (and praise him, still is). Yet it had taken months and sometimes even years to work through the deep cuts with him and be healed. Now as I recalled those who had inflicted these wounds, my first realization dawned: these who had hurt me, by omission and commission, now brought me no fresh pain when I remembered them, for I had forgiven them, every one and every thing. I could and did recall the facts and had memory of the feelings, but I did not enter into them or relive them. God had fully healed me of my hurt, my sorrow, and my self-protection. I was not being ask to re-open healed wounds. Instead I felt another emotion as I remembered; I felt compassion. And, I think, a call to prayer for those who had hurt me.

For myself, as I revisited my own sinfulness, pride, and rebellion, I was not assaulted with fresh guilt and shame. I had been healed too of punishing myself and doing penance. As I remembered, my emotion was sorrow, and again compassion even for my self. I was experiencing God's heart in my behalf, I believe. But I knew that I had long since been forgiven and had been fully released from needing to shame myself.

"Forgetting those things which are behind . . . " Now I felt fresh rejoicing for my cleansing, and no further avoidance. I felt fresh, restored in spirit.

The review of relationships of course included the many loves of my life. I was amazed at how strongly my emotions welled up when I recalled these. The memories were wonderfully vivid; I not only felt the emotions of the encounters, I felt additional emotion in the joy of the memory. My childhood played out in my mind; my mother and my father; siblings down through the years; school days and school mates; boyfriends and girlfriends; the college years; friends of my adulthood, of my teaching years—students and fellow teachers; of my years of leading Bible studies, of colleagues in counseling, of teachers, pastors, new acquaintances: a kaleidoscope of scenes as the benediction of loving poured out.

Scenes of childhood pierced me with their sweetness and poignancy: my bouquet of wildflowers for my mother; my jump into Daddy's arms as he came in the door from work; Mama's hugs; Christmases of scraggy trees and paper cut out decorations; nativity scenes; play with Jerry, my brother, and our little dog, Rags; my second brother Billy, five years younger, in his efforts to talk; burying my little brother Barry's baby feet in the sand (I was seven); the birth of baby sister Rose (so beautiful I was envious) when I was ten; standing with my mother at our front door, thanking God that the war (WWII) had ended; chili hot dog dinners together on Friday nights before we all went together to the football games; family reunions each year at Glenrose in central Texas; all our post-childhood gatherings for holidays and celebrations with all the games and stories and laughter; ties that still bind now so strongly. During my adult years, I said sad good-byes to my brother Bill, my father, and my mother (later this year to my brother Jerry as well), and treasured more greatly those who remained and every sweet addition to the family—the weddings, babies, then more weddings and more babies. I wept glad tears of remembering.

I courageously (I think) visited the old romances, but I am shy to write about them. Yet "the way of a man with a maid" triggered many of the strongest emotions of my life, both glad and sorrowful, but not to be missed in learning the fullness of life nor dismissed from memory.

So I didn't. I revived them, even in the uneven mixture of agony and ecstasy. I was glad I did.

I began to recall friends, one by one, from childhood on down the years. Some came and went; others stayed for our lifetimes, and are still there. Those dearest to my heart, formed from common bonds of Christian love, became dearer during my worst years. Several of these are dead now, and I greatly grieved their going. This one grievous emotion of sorrow over loss returned to me in full force. Yet it was so mingled with the love of the ones I had known that I freshly understood "sorrowful yet always rejoicing," for I had immense joy even in my sorrow as I remembered them.

One of them, Sherry Lee, inspired this next poem, spurred by John 7:37: "Jesus stood and said . . . 'If a man is thirsty, let him come to me and drink. Whoever believes in me, as the Scripture has said, streams of living water will flow from within him.'"

Sister Friend

The bright
white
Love-Light
water of Life
poured into her small frame
and sent forth sprays
of iridescent joy,
melted the ice blue eyes
into pools of compassion,
filled the caverns of creativity
and brought forth
music, laughter, and song,
formed fathomless reservoirs
of wisdom,
sent flowing forth
fountains of understanding

and care,
fashioned wave upon wave
of faithfulness,
faithfulness,
faithfulness, filling the years,
and created currents
of empathy,
mercy,
and love.
Each time I enter these rivers
I come forth
revived,
renewed
refreshed,
enlivened,
encouraged,
blessed.
And blessing, blessing, blessing
God
For all the fullness
that flows
from my sister friend.
Streams without end.
Amen.

I spent a long while remembering those years in the Santa Inez Valley and all the joy of love that grew among us as we ministered and studied together in our women's Bible study. Memory after memory unfolded intertwined with poignant emotion of how we loved, labored, laughed and cried. A few lines of another poem, "Friends," express it as well as I can:

Remembering the golden years,
The glow of shared grace,
The blessed bonds,
Beautiful in the weaving,

Of His hands,
Impossible to sever,
Never subject
To the prey of years or tears . . .

Another lingering came with scenes of my home and children in Anaheim and later in the Santa Inez Valley. I remember one beautiful Sunday: I gathered my step-children into my arms, as they ran to meet me across the church yard. I visited scene after scene of our times of play—so many times, so many places, the beaches, the parks, the camp-outs, the holidays. I remembered the year I hid all their Christmas gifts and wrote clues as where to find them. I don't know (they really had a great good time on their hunt) but I think maybe I had more fun than they did.

I relived with great gladness the birth of my son, his baby years, the toddler, the school boy, the teen, the handsome man. All the love I had felt as I held that precious baby to myself came flowing back, and pierced my heart again in scene after scene as the years flowed by with peaks of love and valleys of trial. Oh how I loved that child, did love, do love, ever shall love.

My list could go on and on into my adult years of teaching, home-making, counseling, each having its own stories of relationships, some to leave sadly, some to keep. I came to the time I retired, severed strong ties, and left my country because I believed God called me out. But then I recalled what awaited me: the more recent incredibly full years of meeting George, our marriage, our travels, forming Canadian ties, my wonderful church, pastors, brothers and sisters there; wonderful people I've counseled; students in the classes I've taught, my neighbors and friends—how rich and loving and full of grace!

All my memories of these loving relationships were filled with unforgettable moments of deep and abiding care, oneness, and sheer happiness. This produced my second realization: I was amazed to find how *many* there were, down through the years and seasons. The realization came that those who loved me were far greater in number than those who had pierced me, and that the blessing of it far outweighed the pain. Ah, think of heaven!

My third realization came with remembering my foremost love down through the years: the Triune God. How awesomely wonderful to recall again special moments encountering his person, his presence, his dealings with me, then and now. Ultimate beauty is this grace abounding. No words can describe the marvel of God's faithfulness as I recalled it through the years.

"Oh God," my heart cried as I completed my assignment, "how precious beyond measure is *loving*! Yours for us, ours for you. And people—my love for them, theirs for me! You gave love to us as a gift, and all the loves between people are from you. How profoundly we are blessed!"

Scriptures flooded my mind: "God has poured out his love into our hearts . . . ";

"Every good and perfect gift is from above, coming down from the Father . . . "; "We love because he first loved us."

Then the remembrance came again of his loving me down through the years. And my increasing love for him.

I thought again of *hesed*, of all the poured out goodness on my life that I had experienced from the three assignments God had given me, grace for my hospital stay. Then this realization came to me, like an immense light had just flashed on: I hadn't even begun to remember on all the rest of my life. I hadn't been asked to. But I began to merely consider in a broad way—all the places, picnics, parades, parties; all big events and mind-bending trips; all the wild adventures and days of play; all the best books and cinematic marvels; all the art and sculpture; all the poetry and plays; all the musicals and theater triumphs; all the cars, boats, planes, and trains; all the gardens and flowers; all the amazing animals; all the daily array of sky and trees and river and lake; all the delicious foods and drinks I've relished; all the clothes and shoes and coats and hats I've owned; all the glorious church services I've attended; all the hymns and songs of praise I've sung; all the great teaching and sermons I've heard; all the ministry I have been given to engage in; all the groups I've been part of; all the incredible people in all the incredible places . . . and . . . and . . . and.

The conclusion startled me as the thoughts came: what a full and wonderful life I have lived! If not one thing were ever added again, how could I ever ask for more? What *grace* I have known! Oh that I might fully realize it and never forget!

CHAPTER TWENTY ONE

DAY BY DAY

My two weeks in the hospital ended. I was weak and fragile, but very glad to be going home. George did all he could to make it that way, and three days later my sister Rose and her husband Doug arrived to take care of me. I didn't need much care, just rest and a little exertion now and then. But their company cheered and exhilarated, full of laughter and Christmas sparkle, while the snow fell, and they delighted in it, being from Texas where snow is rarely seen. My soul was joyful, and my body continued to make an excellent recovery.

Gradually my face took on recognizable proportions as it shrank into place. True, I am left with a rather crooked mouth, uneven jaw line (a piece of bone was removed), slurry speech, limited sense of taste, and some numbness on the left side of my face. I have three missing molars where food loves to hide. My long scar, though, is scarcely noticeable.

So all in all, I have much to be thankful for—I can still eat! And I have no cancer. I am assured it will not return. I'm blessed.

In this last year since my surgery, my kidney function has continued at a low maintenance level, growing slightly better, and my weight has held steady. I have not regained my former vigor so my physical activity is still limited and my energy low. I do have ups and downs both in energy and in mood, and still must arise to fight the fight of faith most days. In my low times, I struggle with my debilitation, longing to be up and doing, but lacking the wherewithal to do much of anything. I wander mentally through a fog, feeling lost and alone. Then I cry to God and lament. But always, after awhile, sometimes long, sometimes short, I rest into him and begin to know his love again. I soak in it awhile until peace comes. Then I realize the treasure he himself is to me personally, and begin to know again immense gratitude for the health I do have, for the innumerable small blessings that come each day, and for a sense of personal enlargement. I realize I can still awake each day to a new day, glad for it, but satisfied to have that one day without counting on tomorrow. I am here for as long as he wants me here, learning to live just as I am, in his company.

I experience my limitations now in many ways. I have almost finished grieving my losses, I think. Perhaps though I won't, this side of heaven. Each new season brings reminders of those things I can no longer engage in, and my sense of loss pervades again. Yet I am profoundly glad for what is left to me and what I have left to learn and to experience.

As I have reviewed all I have written, I conclude that there are two sides to diminishment. On the one side is the sorrow of loss. The counter side adds the blessings of peace, gratitude, awareness, and the increase of loving—the beauties of the last mile home.

Yet inevitably a question comes to mind: What now? Now in my diminished state, what assignment do you have for me, Lord? This inquiry led to Part III, and a surprising revelation.

PART THREE

VISTAS OF JOY

Though outwardly we are wasting away,
yet inwardly we are being renewed day by day.
For our light and momentary troubles are
achieving for us an eternal glory that far outweighs
them all. So we fix our eyes not on what is seen,
but on what is unseen. For what is seen is
temporary, but what is unseen is eternal.
2 Corinthians 4:16-18

CHAPTER TWENTY TWO

A NEW PERSPECTIVE

Since my energy level rises and falls, I pace myself accordingly. I have learned to listen to my body's signal that I have done enough for the time being, and now need to rest awhile. "He makes me lie down in green pastures." (Psalm 23:2) Even when my energy has increased at bit, I have again and again sensed a warning from God to heed what he has taught me through the months of diminishment. I am not to try to resume my former "normal" ways, even when I feel the urge to. In my new mode of living, still diminished, he challenges me to do only what he bids me.

"And what would that be?" I asked a few months ago. This verse came to mind: "Though outwardly we are wasting away, yet inwardly we are being renewed day by day." (2 Corinthians 4:16) I thought again of the learning I had gleaned through the months of diminishment, and the grace I had experienced in the hospital. Yet now I felt a new awareness of challenge, vague and murky but insistent.

As I prayed, I sensed God challenging me in regard to love. I knew well the commands of Jesus, referring to the Torah, to love God with all your heart, soul, mind and strength, and to love your neighbor as yourself. I also recalled his words to the disciples at the last supper—three times—to love one another as he had loved them.

Did my diminishment and ceasing of ministry mean I did not love the Lord or his people as I once had? I didn't think so. Love is not based on the amount of activity, is it?

What was the Lord saying to me? What would he have me do? I found no answers to these questions at that time, so I left the particulars to the Lord to reveal to me in his time, but also set my heart to "love well" with what little energy remained in me.

A few weeks later I was asked to speak for the Women's Ministries at the opening meeting of the fall. I didn't take a minute to consider my low energy level, or wonder if I could effectively speak for the thirty minutes. With complete assurance that God was opening this door to me, I immediately said I would if I could speak on "First Love." I was surprised at myself for answering so quickly and wondered why I had insisted on that topic. I asked the Lord what lay behind it and found myself recalling that famous verse in Revelation where the risen and glorified Jesus speaks to the seven churches, first to the church at Ephesus: "Yet I hold this against you: You have forsaken your first love." (Revelation 2:4) What was this first love in those early Christians? Surely their love for the Savior that poured forth to him when they first received the message of salvation. Their fervor, their passion, their desire was for pleasing their Lord, the bridegroom of the church (see Ephesians 5:31–32). What had happened to this first love?

How did they lose it?

Had I lost mine?

I began to consider my own experience of "first love" with Christ. Over forty years ago, following a sojourn in the pit of despair, I found myself in a new starting-over place, ready to begin my Christian walk all over again. Now a wife, a mother to two step-children, a homemaker, and a faithful member of a local church, I also felt a need for fellowship with women. So I joined a women's Bible study, a large interdenominational one that united women from all the churches of the community, led by a dynamic and very effective teacher, Betty Alexander. There I met not only many wonderful women, but through the study was brought face to face with the author of my salvation, Jesus Christ, in an entirely new encounter.

One day as I meditated on the passage for study, a portion of John I think, I had an overwhelming sense of enlightenment. I had been raised in the church and had long been a believer, yet for the first time ever, I began to fathom the depth of God's love for human beings, and for me particularly. Romans 5:5 tells us, "God has poured out his love into our hearts by the Holy Spirit, whom he has given us." Now it was happening to me! It was as if oceans of love were pouring in on me, as oceans of sorrow and loss poured out—a flushing out, a pouring in. I slid off the sofa, fell to my knees, and then lay flat out on my face. I sobbed and worshipped, dismayed over my sins, yet grasping the truth of my awesome redemption with my whole being, filled with an overwhelming breaking and a simultaneous ecstasy. How much time passed I don't know, but I do know that the experience brought incredible change in me. I was never quite the same again. I now had genuine awareness and experience of the depths of God's love for me, far beyond any love I had ever known. "We love because he first loved us." (1 John 4:19) And oh, what love welled up in me in response!

From that time on I was like a young bride to be, so incredibly fascinated with this perfect Lover that I could never get enough of him. I couldn't stay out of the Bible where I could watch him, listening to all he had to say, wondering at his majesty and wisdom, his love and kindness. I gathered his promises and his plans for me like a bride finding furnishings for her home. Each find delighted me. I couldn't stop extolling him and telling him how much I loved him and how incredible he was—it just poured out of me. My day began on the run, getting all my duties and chores attended to in record time, so I could then open the Book and begin to see and hear him again. My joy was boundless. His love for me and in me was changing me day by day. Every day was beautiful, a new adventure. Every chore was light. Every relationship was affected. Every person gave an opportunity to let my love flow. I felt happily drunk on the new wine of the Spirit.

Down through the years that fountain of first love became a steady river of love in me. I came to know this faithful Lord better and better and so my love for him grew stronger and steadier; the river surged on.

Then came times of trial and sorrow producing a season of doubting that dried up much of my river of faith. What remnants of the river that remained were down and brown and sluggish as a late summer creek. I needed autumn rains. Always they came after a time of repentance and grieving for my weak faith, my blocking the flow of first love. The river surged again.

Decades have passed. I have learned much and certainly that God's love flow to me and in me is never diminished, nor will be, unless I *will* it. And I have so willed it, from time to time, blocking it with my doubts and resentments. Yet I now know I am loved with a love *at all times* as torrentially strong as I experienced that day so long ago. I have only to choose to receive it. I bathe in it.

But after my cancer operation I faced a new reality. In my diminished and weakened state, I felt new threats to my faith as I questioned God's love and goodness for allowing my kidney condition to *remain*. I had gained greatly from having gone through the trials of nephritis and cancer. But I had come through. Why was I still not being healed completely?

My thoughts went back to Richard Miller, a young man I knew almost half a century ago. I was then a member of a singles' Sunday School class. One of our members never attended—Richard. Richard had had polio when he was a child, and as a result both legs were wasted and useless. His arms were also greatly weakened, and he had the use of only two fingers on his right hand. Because of lung damage, he had difficulty breathing and talking. He could sit for only short periods of time. Our whole class would visit him at the facility where he spent the vast majority of his limited life. Yet I had never before nor have I ever since seen anyone who loved the Lord so greatly. His face was radiant, his immense joy evident, his praise and thanksgiving an endless flow. When he had alone times and sufficient energy, he made leather key holders to give away to his friends and to others to express his love in a tangible way. How he did it, I could not imagine, but I was certain it took immense effort for one so limited. I could not fathom, at the time, how he could be so genuinely happy, so truly content, for he obviously didn't force it at all—he literally poured out a love stream effortlessly.

I thought of the recent internet video I had seen of the young evangelist who had no arms or legs who yet joyously proclaimed his message of love. I thought of Joni Erickson whose dive left her a quadriplegic, with only the use of her mouth, yet who spoke, drew, and wrote of her finding an amazingly joyous life and loving through her faith in Jesus. I thought of my mother in her 90's, bed-ridden, almost blind, terribly frail and weak, yet greeting her attendants with love every day, inquiring about their families, praying for them—she genuinely cared. She never failed to encourage them to have faith in her Savior. There are others I could recall—these fountains of living water that were and are filled and over-flowing with the "first love" even with immense diminishment that was never healed.

Where was that fountain in me? Did I now use my lack of energy as an excuse for lack of fervent love? Now, in my continuing trials and loss, was I doubting God again?

CHAPTER TWENTY THREE

BEHOLD

How was it then, that having known "first love" and having continued in it, that I could now, with the on-going trial of diminishment, begin to doubt again his goodness?

I think that most of us, when we first come to know the Lord, are incredulous at the magnitude of his overall plan. When we get a firm grasp of all God has done in creating and redeeming and planning for the future of his beloved mankind, we are overwhelmed, as I was on my "first love" day. It is too good to be believed. The indwelling of the Trinity astounds us. That the God of the universe would take up residence in each of us is personally dumbfounding. If we open ourselves to believe, the Holy Spirit begins to "guide . . . into all truth" as Jesus said he would. We are experiencing spiritual love, a whole new dimension of living.

The love of God for us as now revealed far surpasses any human love we have ever experienced, no matter how pure and dear, and indeed seems to be a profound composite of all the loves we have ever known or needed while at the same time exceeds any of them: parent love, love of a friend, love of a spouse, love of children, love of a hero, love of a leader, love of a teacher, all, all, in One. " . . . God has poured out his love into our hearts by the Holy Spirit, whom he has given us." (Romans 5:5) If open to it, we are deluged by it. But then . . . Is your story like mine?

Trials come. Sorrows abound. Misunderstandings, rejections, job failures, health impairments, stresses and strains of marriage, parenting, church life, unaided ministries, a list unending. The fight of faith is unceasing. We grow weary. We grow discouraged. We have tried so hard . . .

For most, I think, and for me, that was the major problem. When I was deluged by this first love, I knew I just received it. I did nothing to earn it, nor could I. But as time went by I went back to the human system of believing no one, and so Christ as well, would keep on loving me or approving of me unless I performed well enough, unless I kept the rules, unless I began to *prove my* value. I didn't know I was doing this, but beyond my conscious thinking, my old habits of responding began to assert themselves. How insidious this lie based on my own sense of lack of worth, of shame for being of such little value, the lie that I must now return to earning favor.

My feelings seemed to spring from assignments I laid on myself: I must read so much Scripture each day, pray a set amount, tithe, attend church regularly, join a program of evangelism, witness to my neighbor, join every church project, help clean up after every church supper, keep the nursery or teach children's Sunday school—the list kept lengthening. But one day I couldn't keep juggling it all; I was getting exhausted. I felt huge failure. Why keep trying? I knew I'd never be able to do enough; I would never get it right.

Yet Scripture told me: "As you have therefore received Christ Jesus the Lord, so walk in him." (Colossians 2:6)

Sure, sure, walk in the Spirit; I know, I know! I'm trying to! Trying. Yet old patterns crept in.

Here's another: if I was not burned out by trying to do good works and if I had plenty of energy, I would then take the opposite detour away from grace: I would get spellbound by my own good works. Deeper than I consciously registered, born of my insecurity, striving to be good enough emerged; then out of that striving came many good works to prove my worth; then out of my accomplishments, pride grew like an unpruned tree. I didn't see it at the time; few do, I think. We are all subject to drifting back to the old ways of earning worth, motivated by an innate shame that we are naked sinners.

Of course, it isn't just God we seek to impress. We have lived for so long registering both consciously and subconsciously the reactions and responses of others that we are super sensitive to them. Our emotions, moods, and attitudes rise and fall in response. How do *they* like it? What do *they* think? Surely they wouldn't like me if they could see me as I really am. I will hide behind my title, my skill, my appearance, my work, my home, my possessions, my children, my knowledge, my intelligence,—my, my, my. How many hats can I wear? How many roles can I play? How many people can I fool?

Oh to see, once for all, that I have all I ever need to please God *in Christ*. And no one else's opinion counts! Not that I am seeking to displease them, but neither can I let their opinions deter me from doing his will. I have only to join my heart to Jesus, for he loves me; his Spirit will direct me, energize me, pull me into his word, give me delight in prayer, pour love of others into me and through me. As always, it is all his work *in me.* He works as I will am willing to receive his will and his work in and through me: "continue to work out your salvation with fear and trembling. For it is God who works in you to will and to act according to his good purpose." (Philippians 2:12-13)

Paul concludes Chapter 11 in the book of Romans with a mighty doxology:

> Oh, the depth of the riches of the wisdom and knowledge of God!
> How unsearchable his judgments, and his paths beyond tracing
>   out!
> "Who has known the mind of the Lord?
> Or who has been his counselor?
> Who has ever given to God that God should repay him?"
> For *from him and through him, and to him are all things.*
> *To him be the glory forever!*
> Amen. (Romans 11:33-36, emphasis mine)

That's it. That's the only way! All things are from, through, and to him. "Christ in me"! Oh to hold fast to it! How this union with him delights! And releases from all that striving. I do not *press* to accomplish; I *flow* in the love stream of the Holy Spirit.

But you know how it is. I hit another snag. I began to realize that sometimes I did not *feel* the degree of love for my beloved Jesus that I formerly had. How could I respond to him without the first love passion? How could I respond to him on days I was low? flat? in stretches of time that I had no energy and no emotion?

I now have less than a third of the energy I would have had, had my kidneys continued to function in a healthy fashion. I am, quite literally, tired most of the time. Does this dampen my emotions? I can only assume it does, for they are often "flat"—nothing moves me much. This grieves me greatly. At those times I can *think* appreciation, love, concern, sadness, compassion, and frustration. But I don't *feel* them as I once did. I somehow experience them in the depths of my being—I know them there and my heart is moved, but I cannot register them *emotionally* as I used to. How odd!—to know that I love my Lord, but to feel no passion. It makes my heart ache!

As I meditated before the Lord about these facts, I came to the conclusion that I had *relied* on emotion to convince myself that I loved him. Ah, another lie uncovered! Again I heard the answer: "Christ in you, the hope of glory"—a union of my spirit with his Spirit, a union of *spirits* whether my emotions are stirred or not. The better I come to know him, the fuller is this union, and the stronger I experience it spiritually.

How well do I *now* know and love Jesus Christ? I pondered my answer.

In the past I read my Bible with diligence. I learned how God interacted with man as I studied the Old Testament. I meditated on the wonder of Christ's incarnation, life, teaching, death, resurrection and ascension in the New Testament. I poured over the apostles' letters. In all my studies and "beholding" of the Lord, I would ask myself, "What does this mean to me and for me?" I wanted to know God and to please him, yes, because I loved him, but mainly I think because I knew it was the best course of action for me in a difficult world. Sometimes the question extended to "What's best for us?" meaning marriage, or family, or friends, or church, or occasionally the country or the world. But the focus was mainly on myself, I think. I wanted to learn, to do well, to shine in God's eyes. Then as I began to mature and behold more acutely, I began to learn to focus more on the Lord himself. His character and nature became more and more apparent. His person became real to me as I dwelt with him in the gospels, probed truths of him in Paul's letters, and joined to adore him throughout the scriptures. I began to *know him*, not just know about him. This is the one who now indwells me, and I sense his presence.

Often as I now read of his actions in the scriptures, I ask, "What did this mean to the Lord?" How did he feel and think and respond as he did all he did? I ask the Spirit to bring each incident fully to life as I focus on Jesus. For instance, in the past I have been greatly moved to watch Jesus restore sight to the man born blind (see John, Chapter 4). I was thrilled to see him act in this man's behalf and to know he was the God who cared to open my eyes to see fully too. But now as I read the encounter, I am moved to focus almost entirely on Jesus. With what feeling did he reach to this man, and what did it mean to Jesus to form clay and anoint the man's eyes, knowing if the man obeyed him and went and washed, he would have his sight? The Holy Spirit moves in my heart to take me into the heart of Jesus, even when my emotions aren't greatly engaged. I can *know* with heart knowledge, for I have been given the "mind of Christ."

A fresh realization strikes me: Now, in my weariness, in my diminishment, I am longing to come into a deeper, fuller, wider, higher love *relationship* with my beloved Lord than I have ever known. Is this because, with outer life now so greatly curtailed, I have time and focus for the inner life? Can I become more attentive, listening longer, more deeply to his voice? Do I yearn to hear him more acutely in the Word, sense his presence more keenly, take time to abide in him more fully? Sometimes yes, sometimes no. It is easy to grab for distractions so that I don't register my weariness. It wears on me, and I want to avoid it. Yet distractions never satisfy; I need relationship. I do know that I love to sit in silence with him, absorbing his love for me, responding to my Beloved.

A wonderful question came to mind one day as I sat with him, delighting in him: What in me gives delight to God? What ways particularly give *him* pleasure? I looked to find in Scripture all the expressions of the delight of God, his pleasure, his joy. Lovers delight in giving delight to those they love. He gave and gives immeasurable delight to me. I longed to give delight to him.

Pleasure, please, delight, joy, enjoy—I looked up all the references I could find.

I hit treasure, of course.

CHAPTER TWENTY FOUR

GOD OF DELIGHT

How do you think of God? What impression do you have of him? I asked myself these questions.

When we become aware from the Bible record of the whole scope of God's plan concerning the creation of man and the earth within the span of time, we see a God who experiences *delight*. Nowhere, I think, do we get a better understanding of this awesome plan of the joyous Creator than in the book of Ephesians. Paul outlines God's design and intention in the first chapter:

> Praise be to the God and Father of our Lord Jesus Christ, who blessed us in the heavenly realms with every spiritual blessing in Christ. For he chose us in him before the creation of the world to be holy and blameless in his sight. In love he predestined us to be adopted as his sons through Jesus Christ, in accordance with his *pleasure* and will—to the praise of his glorious grace, which he has freely given us in the One he loves. In him we have redemption through his blood, the

forgiveness of sins, in accordance with the riches of God's grace that he lavished on us with all wisdom and understanding. And he made known to us the mystery of his will according to his good *pleasure*, which he purposed in Christ, to be put into effect when the times will have reached their fulfillment—to bring all things in heaven and on earth together under one head, even Christ. (Ephesians 1:3–10, emphasis mine)

Clearly, to create man and to redeem him was already in God's mind before the creation of the earth, the planet designed to be man's dwelling place. Christ was "the lamb slain before the foundation of the world." (Revelation 8:13) May I grasp hold of all this Ephesians chapter unfolds to its readers. May I fully understand what Paul declares in his letter to the Colossians: speaking of Christ, "all things were made by him and *for* him." I find it incredible to think how much pleasure it gave the Triune God to unfold this plan: to have us, to save us, to relate to us eternally. I have long been astounded at the scope of it all, but never before have I considered the *joy* it gave to God.

Proverbs 8:30–31 gives a vivid picture of the creating Christ. Here Wisdom, personified as a woman, speaks of the creation of earth and man:

> Then I was the craftsman at his side
> I was filled with delight day after day,
> rejoicing always in his presence,
> rejoicing in his whole world
> and *delighting* in mankind. (emphasis mine)

I recall that God, after each day of creation described in Genesis, declared that it was *good*, and then on the sixth day, "And God saw everything that he had made, and behold, it was very good." (Genesis 1:3) Imagine his pleasure!

As I meditate on the beginning of God's act of creating, I consider how the Godhead desired relationship with these humans. What astounds me most is this: the Trinity had already determined to do everything necessary to bring them into that relationship, holy and blameless, by means of Christ's death. I also remember what we are told in Hebrews: "Let us fix our eyes on Jesus, the author and perfecter of our faith, who for the *joy* set before him endured the cross, despising the shame, and sat down at the right hand of the throne of God." (Hebrews 12:2, emphasis mine) What joy was set before him? Surely this longed for relationship with human beings, now made open.

David knew this God of joy and delight as he fellowshipped with him. What a closeness of intimacy, what heart to heart relationship:

> You have made known to me the path of life;
> you will fill me with joy in your presence,
> with eternal pleasures at your right hand. (Psalm 16:11)

All through the Old Testament we see the God of Creation moving to bring his ultimate over-arching plan to fulfillment. "But when the time had fully come, God sent his Son, born of a woman, born under law, to redeem those under law, that we might receive the full rights of sons. Because you are sons, God sent the Spirit of his Son into our heart, the Spirit who calls out 'Abba, Father.'" (Galatians 4:4-5) How heaven rejoiced at the Savior's birth! How the angels sang! And the Father—was he delighted that night? More than we can possibly comprehend, I think.

How marvelous to hear the Father proclaim his delight in his Son as Jesus was baptized and began his earthly ministry: "And a voice came from heaven: 'You are my Son, whom I love; with you I am *well pleased.*'" (Luke 3:22, emphasis mine) How similar were his words at the Transfiguration: "While he was still speaking, a bright cloud enveloped them, and a voice from the cloud said, 'This is my Son, whom I love; with him I am well pleased. Listen to him!'" (Matthew 17:5, emphasis mine)

What joy did Jesus know as he listened to the Father and moved in the power of the Spirit as he proclaimed and taught, announcing and ushering in the kingdom? Think how the Trinity rejoiced when he fed the thousands, healed all who came to him, raised the dead! Hear again some of his statements:

"I tell you that in the same way there will be more *rejoicing* in heaven over one sinner who repents than over ninety-nine righteous persons who do not need to repent." (Luke 15:7, emphasis mine)

"Do not be afraid, little flock, for your Father has been pleased to give you the kingdom." (Luke 12:32, emphasis mine)

To his disciples after teaching them of abiding in him, of his Father's love for them, and of their need to obey because of their love for him: "I have told you this so that my *joy* may be in you and that your *joy* may be complete." (John 15:11, emphasis mine)

On that last night just before he was arrested, he prayed to the Father: "I am coming to you now, but I say these things while I am still in the world, so that they may have the full measure of my *joy* within them." (John 17:13, emphasis mine) These things? I need to meditate deeply on John 13–17.

What is God's delight?—that we might *experience his joy!*

Consider the counter side—the grief he felt and now feels when ignored, rejected, and scorned. In the Old Testament we see that God laments long and frequently over the deafness and waywardness of Israel; how they stoned the prophets and refused to be warned. See Jesus: "As he approached Jerusalem and saw the city, he wept over it and said, 'If you, even you had only known on this day, what would bring you peace—but now it is hidden from you eyes.'" (Luke 19:41)

Often I sense a very deep sorrow, beyond the realm of surface emotion and tears, a bowing down grief within me, when I consider the current state of the world. Such blindness to the true nature of

God abounds. Such arrogance and pride in the reasoning of man. Such incredible faith in the discoveries of science that are as yet very limited. I grieve for the darkness of the lost. I was once there, and how bleak and dark it was! A twilight zone. How truly broad is the road that leads to destruction, and how very many travel that road, never realizing the wonder of life itself and all the love that God pours onto them in his never-ending lovingkindness day after day. I believe I am grieving with God at those times.

Yet the joy side prevails to those who open to it.

Speaking of Christ we read, "Yet to all who received him, to those who believed in his name, he gave the right to become children of God . . . born of God. (John 1:12) In Christ's parable, we see the good shepherd leave the ninety and nine, and pursue the one lost one. Does God delight in his children?

> "The Lord your God is with you,
> he is mighty to save.
> He will take *great delight* in you,
> he will quiet you with his love,
> he will rejoice over you with singing."
> (Zephaniah 3:17, emphasis mine)

How richly he provides for their joy: he not only "richly provides us with everything for our enjoyment" (I Timothy 6:17), but also "has given us everything we need for life and godliness through our knowledge of him"(2 Peter 1:3)—that would be an incredible list of wonders of salvation and his indwelling.

I recall again his overflowing *hesed*. Do I fail to realize daily the rich delight of his presence, his guidance, his care, his companioning? Only if I choose to. He is indeed the God who *enjoys* giving joy to his children.

As he delights me in loving me, so I would delight him. Paul said it to the Corinthians, "So we make it our goal to please him. (2 Corinthians 5:9) Paul also told the Colossians: " . . . we have not stopped praying for you, and asking God to fill you with the knowledge of his will through all spiritual wisdom and understanding. And we pray this in order that you may live a life worthy of the Lord and may please him in every way; bearing fruit in every good work, growing in the knowledge of God." (Colossians 1:9–10) So I pray, "Lord, teach me how to please and delight you, even now in the years of diminishment."

CHAPTER TWENTY FIVE

DELIGHTING GOD

I f I can no longer delight God in the ways I used to, lacking the energy to minister as I once did, then what now *can* I do? As I studied the subject, I found God is clearly *pleased* by certain habits of those who say they love him, habits implanted and empowered by the Holy Spirit, habits still possible to the diminished person, habits of attitude and thought as well as action, primarily habits of relating to him.

What habits delight God? I often remember the line in the movie, *Chariots of Fire*, when Eric Liddell explains to his sister why he runs: "I know God made me for a missionary. But he also made me fast. And when I run, I feel his pleasure!" Can you feel God's pleasure when you do certain things you are sure he wants? We can be certain we give him pleasure in ways the scriptures declare.

I have organized what I found into six major categories. Much has been written about each one, and I will not try to probe the depths of any. I want mainly to point to those *habits of relating to him* that delight his heart.

1. Listening to God and being open to his leading.

There is no appeal made more frequently by the prophets than to listen to God, to hear him and heed him. How they cried out to the people, pleading for them to heed the words of God as they quoted him and to accept his warnings. How tragic that most of the people did not. I think the most eloquent plea in the Old Testament pours from God himself. It is found in Psalms 81 where the psalmist puts forth God's own heart and anguish:

> " . . . if you would but listen to me,
> O, Israel!
> But my people would not listen to
> me;
> Israel would not submit to me . . .
> If my people would but listen to me,
> if Israel would follow my ways,
> how quickly would I subdue their
> enemies
> and turn my hand against their foes!"

At the transfiguration of Christ, a voice came from the bright cloud that enveloped Peter, James, and John. Hear the Father speaking (a verse I have previously quoted, but now with a different emphasis), "This is my Son, whom I love, with him I am well pleased. *Listen to him!*" (Matthew 17:5, emphasis mine) How can we miss the fact that God is pleased when we listen to him gratefully, with full and sustained attention.

How do we hear? By being attentive to the voice of the Holy Spirit as he speaks into our hearts and minds. Most particularly the Spirit speaks to us through the scriptures as we listen to all he has to reveal. Jesus spoke words directly to the people as he taught; we receive them from the pages in the Gospels that record them. What a delighted prayer he prayed, "I praise you, Father, Lord of heaven and earth, because you have hidden these things from the wise and learned, and revealed them to little children. Yes, Father, for this was your good *pleasure.*" (Luke 10:21, emphasis mine) I conclude that the Lord is still delighted to open the revelation to us when our hearts are tuned to hear. Recall Ephesians 1:9 "And he made known to us the mystery of his will according to his good *pleasure* . . . " (emphasis mine)

It's clear all through the Bible that God wants to be heard. Can you identify with this longing? Have you ever longed to be listened to and understood? Can you recall how you felt when you were ignored or spurned or told you didn't know what you were talking about? On the other hand, can you remember longing to pour out your heart on a matter? When you found a caring listener and could speak freely for as long as you desired, how did you feel then? For myself, at those times when I am truly heard, I experience a deep and great satisfaction, a profound joy. So does God.

Do I give God that immense pleasure of being heard? Am I slow to open the Book? Do I feel I already know it? Do I speed read its pages? Or do I continue to give time for the Spirit to give illumination and to give application to me personally? Am I further attentive to the voice of the Holy Spirit as he gives me words of guidance beyond those of Scripture but always in line with them? Do I pray to know God's will, then fail to listen to what he wants? Do I pray for others and fail to seek his heart's desire for them? Do I grieve God in how I listen to him? Amazing but true that I can give him joy or tears in how I listen. Which will it be?

Diminishment does not curtail my listening to God. Since I now have fewer activities and more time, my limitations may even increase my listening to him. I may not be as alert as I once was, but if I am willing, I certainly can give him the delight of the open ear.

2. Prayer

Closely related to hearing God is our speaking to him. Whatever form it takes, God is delighted to listen to his children. "but the prayer of the upright pleases him." (Proverbs 15:8) The many forms of prayer may open to wider and fuller experience of him, and each gives him the pleasure of our company. Let me focus on just three.

"Trust in him at all times, O people; pour out your hearts to him, for our God is a refuge." (Psalm 62:8) Just as a mother longs for her hurting child to pour out his anguish to her, that she might comfort and counsel him, so our parent God longs for his children to come to him. The writer of Hebrews assures us: "For we do not have a high priest who is unable to sympathize with our weaknesses, but we have one who has been tempted in every way, just as we are—yet without sin." (Hebrews 4:15) This high priest is Jesus, who now by his indwelling Spirit, assures us that we will be listened to and understood, loved and comforted. "Let us then approach the throne of grace with confidence, so that we may receive mercy and find grace to help us in out time of need." (Hebrews 4:16) Do I please him by doing so—by coming and pouring out my heart? The invitation is so very clear—from Christ himself: "Come unto me, all you who are weary and burdened, and I will give you rest." (Matthew 11:28) He longs for me to come. Why do I hesitate and nurse my negative feelings and thoughts instead? Not only do I cheat myself but I deny him the deep pleasure it gives him to minister to his child.

Besides "pouring out prayers" I frequently pray prayers of petition. How often Jesus bids his followers to ask of God! All right, I do. But then sometimes I don't get answers. Why not? Well, of course there is my selfish desire to have what I want. That he will not give me, for he would be a poor parent if he did. "When you ask, you do not receive, because you ask with wrong motives that you may spend what you get on your pleasures." (James 4:3) What then should I ask to receive? I should ask for what I *need*.

Most of us, I think, focus on material, financial, and health needs. These may not be primary but are pressing, and Jesus tells us to ask in regard to them. Yet again, Jesus assures us that the Father knows what we need before we ask him. Why then would he have us ask? We ask because it delights him that we realize he is the giver, that "Every good and perfect gift is from above, coming down from the Father of the heavenly lights . . . " (James 1:17) It delights him for us to realize he is the source and supplier of *all* we need. We ask so that we may be open to and aware of his lovingkindness and be blessed by it, receivers rather than graspers. So we ask forthrightly with confidence in his love and graciousness. He is the generous compassionate God who takes joy in giving, and delights to be asked.

Beyond asking for my material and body and soul needs as I perceive them, I ask God for the many spiritual aspects of my life, for they are eternally significant, as I see it. My life is lived out of the union of my spirit with the Holy Spirit; all my resources and supply originate there. (See Paul's prayers for believers in Ephesians, Philippians, and Colossians.) I ask for more love for Christ, more conformity to him, more understanding of him and his will, for insight into the Scripture, for growth and enlargement, for increased love of others, for protection from temptation, for forgiveness, for endurance and patience and perseverance. The list goes on and on. I ask without hesitation as I become aware of my need. He is delighted to hear my requests, for it is his desire to conform me to the image of Christ.

I encounter another problem in prayer: intercession—when I ask on behalf of others. When I see or hear of their needs, I turn to God with an appeal for help. But do I ask what I want for them, or do I seek his will for them? Do I open my heart to his heart, even if I do not clearly discern his will? I do not always know the answers to these questions. How does God hear my prayers? If I am motivated by love and also by a longing that his will be done and that he be glorified, I believe he is pleased to hear my prayers.

Does God answer these prayers? Well, first, am I trusting him to answer? Am I listening for his answer? I have said sometimes he doesn't answer from my point of view, but in truth he always does answer. Sometimes soon; sometimes late. Sometimes with a clear yes; sometimes with a no; sometimes with "Trust me"; sometimes in a way very unlike I expected. Are these not the ways that loving parents answer their children? Yet the good parent welcomes the request of his child and the trust that the asking shows.

But beyond pouring out, asking, and interceding, do I share experiences with God as my dearest companion? Do I share my joys? Is our intimacy such that I can share *anything* with him? Do I give him pleasure by doing so? Clearly, my willingness to pray, to commune, to fellowship, to ask, to adore, to meditate, to engage in any and all kinds of prayer gives him pleasure. No wonder we are told to "pray continually". (1 Thessalonians 5:17) I would give him delight by doing so.

Also, I do not find prayer separate from listening to him. I ask him questions; I listen for answers. As I listen, I dialogue with him in regard to what I am hearing; that's how good relationships are. We spend time together, work together, look and take in life together, read together, rest back and just enjoy together. I'm thankful and I tell him so, and he appreciates my thankfulness. I relish this friendship we have, this union we enjoy, above all things. Listening and prayer are interwoven.

3. *Trust*

"And without faith it is impossible to please God, because anyone who comes to him must believe that he exists and that he rewards those who earnestly seek him." (Hebrews 11:6) The author of Hebrews also quotes from the Old Testament: "But my righteous one will live by faith/ And if he shrinks back, I will not be pleased with him." (Hebrews 10:38) How delighted God is when we trust him, when we know every word of promise will be fulfilled, and we live accordingly. He will do what he says he will do. Back to the subject of listening to him—do I truly believe what he tells me? Do I truly believe in his love for me, in his wisdom, in his commands, in his over-arching plan for mankind, in his guidance of my life?

How often do I decide to trust him, only to take back the control again and do it my own way? There are myriads of ways in which we reveal our lack of trust. I ask him to reveal by his Spirit those ways in which I grieve him with *my* lack of trust. Anxiety, doubt, worry, fret, frustration, useless agonizing over decisions, pursuit of selfish pleasures, the effort to control, to rescue, to change others—all these and more show I trust *me* and seek to control my life for *myself.* As a result, foolish suffering is usually my dividend. It is one thing to say I believe him, and quite another to live out that belief. Shall I literally believe he will supply my needs? Don't I need to strategize, to manipulate, to control? He says I don't.

Shall I literally do what he asks me to do, trusting him for the outcome? Do I insist that I see a good result before I take action as he has directed?

I have to set my mind and heart to trust him! I pray that the Spirit will draw me up short and convict me every time I begin to fail to trust. I know that trust brings me peace and stability, serenity and well-being; I also know that it delights my Lord, and that I long to do.

As with listening and responding, so trust is bound up in all aspects of my relationship with God, as it is with every good relationship.

4. Complete Receptivity

I find this item hard to describe. I perceive it as an attitude of heart toward the Lord, an openness to receive all the teaching, all the insight, all the awareness that creates closeness and intimacy in the relationship. The believer becomes one in heart with God and his purposes, sure of God's leading and desires for him. But it is far more than this. There is a *union* here that transcends awareness in the conscious mind, a deep and growing oneness of "Christ in you, the hope of glory." (Colossians 1:27) It is a union of spirits—mine in his—that defies description. I must lose my solitary self in this union: "For whoever wants to save his life will lose it, but whoever loses his life for me will save it," Jesus tells us. (Luke 9:24)

David had such union in heart with God. In the book of Acts we hear Stephen recalling the history of Israel and her heroes, speaking of God's actions: "After removing Saul, he made David their king. He testified concerning him: 'I have found David son of Jesse a man after my own heart; he will do everything I want him to do.'" (Acts 13:22)

David responded to this most intimate of relationships with God and wrote in his psalms:

> He brought me out into a spacious place
> he rescued me because he delighted in me. (2 Samuel 22:20)

After sinning grievously, David was deeply chastened and repentant and open to all God had to say to him. He was confident, being fully open to God's rebuke and instruction, that he would know all God wanted him to realize:

Surely you desire truth in the inner parts;
you teach me wisdom in the inmost parts. (Psalm 51:6)

As I listen, pray, trust, I experience more and more fully this union with him, this being *in* him. I yearn for it to grow, and it does grow. I think of newlyweds as they learn this harmonizing with each other. When this union is present in any marriage, each carries the beloved in his/her heart so that even when alone, the sense of the spouse's presence pervades the thoughts and decisions. The longing to know, to please, to be in union is ever more present. I treasure this with the Lord when I read his word, when I pray, when I worship, but also in the moments of my day—as I shop for groceries, choose books to read, take a time out for a cup of tea, fold laundry, in all the small things; how precious the union! My receptivity to his constant presence, to our love relationship, gives him joy. I know it gives me joy as well.

5. Obedience

Jesus said very directly, "Why do you call me 'Lord, Lord,' and do not do what I say?" (Luke 6:46) Two questions press: Do I know what he has commanded? Do I obey?

In our union with God, our love for God produces receptivity to Scripture and to those inner revelations that come to us personally from the Lord. If we trust him, we heed him, and *act* on what we are hearing. " . . . continue to work out your own salvation with fear and trembling, for it is God who works in you to will and to act according to his good *pleasure*." (Philippians 2:12-13, emphasis mine)

If I know what he would have me be, will I be it? If I know what he would have me do, will I do it? Similarly, if I know what he would not have me be or do, will I refrain from being it or doing it? These questions, of course, apply to my thoughts and attitudes, as well as my actions. Obviously, if it delights God to have me be receptive to him, it surely increases his delight when I obey.

My thoughts in this regard are as follows: When you love someone, you are eager to delight the beloved. If your mother asks you to do something for her, do you do it? You love her, so if her request is beneficial to her, you will certainly be agreeable. You don't consider it burdensome, or a duty you resent; you are pleased to do as she requests. Jesus felt this way in regard to his Father: " . . . I always do what pleases him." (John 8:29) He explained clearly that this kind of obedience is based on love and gives delight: "As the Father has loved me, so have I loved you. Now remain in my love. If you obey my commands, you will remain in my love, just as I have obeyed my Father's commands and remain in his love. I have told you this so that my joy may be in you and that your *joy* may be complete." (John 15:9-11, emphasis mine)

In regard to God, he doesn't ask us to obey him to burden us, but to benefit us. When we choose to do what he requests, we know it is for our good. When Moses gave God's laws to Israel, he admonished the people: "Acknowledge and take to heart this day that the Lord is God in heaven above and on the earth below. There is no other. Keep his decrees and commands, which I am giving you today, so that it may go well with you and your children after you and that you may live long in the land the Lord you God gives you for all time." (Deuteronomy 4:39-40)

Consider these verses:

"And we pray this in order that you may live a life worthy of the Lord and may please him in every way . . . " (Colossians 1:10)

"So we make it our goal to please him." (2 Corinthians 5:9)

" . . . but he delights in those whose ways are blameless." (Proverbs 11:20)

" . . . but he delights in men who are truthful." (Proverbs 12:22)

" . . . a good soldier . . . wants to please his commanding officer." (2 Timothy 2:3,4)

" . . . and find out what pleases the Lord." (Ephesians 5:10)

"If anyone loves me, he will obey my teaching." (John 14:23)

In these and in many other verses in Scripture, it is clear: God loves to see obedience in his children; it pleases him deeply. For he loves us; he longs for us to have the very best. If we are instructed in Scripture, how quickly our hearts should respond with a ready *YES*, rather than our doubting the instruction, finding fault with it, procrastinating in regard to it, or simply ignoring it. How quickly we should practice obedience until the habits are fixed, and how quickly we should heed the voice of the Spirit however and whenever we perceive him. Our *motivation* to obey is that it benefits us, yes; but more importantly, I believe, is that it gives delight and pleasure to God.

I believe this especially applies to his command to love one another. Does this mean we must memorize and make habits of all the multitude of instructions we find in Scripture? Yes, indeed, we do well to study and memorize and come to know all the myriad ways we need to obey the expressed will of God, but genuinely and from the heart, not mechanically. More importantly, we need to look to the true motivation for obedience: we love him.

We hear the plea of Christ to his disciples as he shared the last supper with them. Three times he exhorted them to love one another:

"A new command I give you: Love one another. As I have love you, so you must love one another. By this all men will know that you are my disciples, if you love one another." (John 13:34-35)

"My command is this: Love each other as I have loved you." (John 15:12)

"This is my command: Love each other." (John 15:17)

Equally it is clear that if we do not heed this and his other commands we do not love him:

"If you love me, you will obey what I command." (John 14:15)

"Whoever has my commands and obeys them, he is the one who loves me." (John 14:21)

"If anyone loves me, he will obey my teaching. My Father will love him, and we will come to him and make our home with him. He who does not love me will not obey my teaching." (John 14:23-24)

Our obedience springs from the deep love we have for our Lord, just as his sprang from his immense love of the Father when he walked the earth. It doesn't end there. We don't just yearn to please the Beloved; we act; we do it. Our obedience does not depend on our own willingness, resolve, and strength, for the promised Holy Spirit abides in us to enable us, but we must be willing to obey. Am I?

When we read Christ's teachings, the writings of Paul, and those of Peter, the ways of this love for one another are clearly spelled out. We are told specifically how love behaves. The command instructs our behavior as we draw on the Holy Spirit for God's love so that we *may* act in love to one another. We realize that kindness springs from this loving, as well as tenderness, graciousness, generosity, forgiveness, encouragement, strengthening, warning, forbearing, truthfulness, honesty, and a host of other traits and behaviors as well. At every moment of loving, the Spirit provides direction and enablement as we are *willing to receive it*.

What about the instructions telling us what to avoid? We read them in the scriptures and also hear them recalled in our minds, as the Holy Spirit directs us.

At any given moment of relationship, we *can know* the way of love; we have only to listen and to heed the Spirit to know it. Whether we obey at that moment is our choice, but the way of obedience is clear.

Is your problem with this the same as mine? I often just react, not waiting to hear or heed the Spirit. I need all his strength first to halt my reaction. He gives it, as I am willing to have it. Then if I will listen, I will be clear about what *to do*. Now to practice! As we exercise in setting our hearts on pleasing God by loving, we find the habits forming. becoming ingrained, both to do, and to refrain from doing. As we learn obedience and practice it, we experience that double portion: we please God, and we are very pleased.

As usual, though, I now have another problem. Many of my active *habits* of loving action have gone by the wayside. For me, the strength for loving in ways I have previously expressed it is often lacking; I simply don't have the energy to do what I once did. But I am learning that love is still possible and new ways of expressing it can be learned and must be learned.

I am realizing more and more that Christ in me loves just through his mere presence. My being with someone, caring, listening, speaking, praying—these are the ways of love. Though I am diminished, I am enlarged in heart and intent if I am willing to learn. This is an on-going process.

For instance, my husband George has become quite hard of hearing, and even though he has hearing aids, he often isn't wearing them for one reason or another. My normal way of speaking to him isn't heard. With my lack of strength and with the difficulty of talking because of my mouth reconstruction, I find speaking effortful at the best of times. Trying to make a deaf person hear is especially draining. At first, after my cancer operation, it made me very frustrated that George didn't hear. "If he would only listen more closely!" I thought. But nothing changed. The situation grew worse. I had to change. I found myself learning to pray at the moment of frustration, pouring out my problem to the Lord, relinquishing it to him, and then waiting and listening for his instruction. And it came: "Position yourself first. Stand or sit close to him when you speak, look at him directly, then speak each word distinctly but not over loudly." I do not mean that these were the words of God spoken to me. No, these were the words in my head, but I believe God put them there! God uses the mind! Also, it was not that I did what I thought immediately. I had to slow down, pray for grace, and then obey the instructions. But in time I have learned to do so (much of the time), and it's better. I think we both have learned increased graciousness and dependence on the Lord.

Obedience gives opportunity to experience the mutual delight I spoke of, and therefore leads to another composite item: praise, worship, and thanksgiving. When I obey readily, I am thankful I did and praise him for the Spirit's work in me, and that gives more pleasure to God.

6. Praise, worship, and thanksgiving.

Just because I have named this item last does not mean it is least in importance. Adoration is vital to each believer's relationship with the Lord. And whenever we praise, worship, and give thanks, God is delighted.

How spiritedly we sing in my church on Sunday mornings, enjoying the music, the rhythm and the words of the songs we sing. Is this praise? Is it worship? Is it thanksgiving? That depends on each individual. What is the motivation? the intention?

Jesus told the Samaritan woman that those who worship must worship "in Spirit and in truth." (ref. John 4) So as God looks on the heart, what does he see? hear? know? Clearly, God responds:

> I will praise God's name in song and glorify him with
> thanksgiving.
> This will *please* the Lord more than an ox
> more than a bull with its horns and hoofs.
> (Psalm 69:30-31, emphasis mine)

In Psalm 149, following the description of joyous singing and worship and dancing, we read these words:

> For the Lord takes *delight* in his people. (Psalm 149:4, emphasis mine)

All through the psalms the singers are exhorted to give thanks and praise to God. Hardly a psalm in the entire psalter fails to exhort praise to God or give praise to God.

But once a week corporate praise, even if incredibly genuine, is not enough. It falls far short of the praise and blessing of the Almighty that should be pouring from us all through each day. Praise and thanksgiving should rise like a waterspout, recurring like Old Faithful, throughout our day. The more alert we become to the Lord's goodness, the more the fountain surges up and sprays forth.

When Paul exhorts us to pray continually, he isn't thinking of our sending out a stream of complaints or pleas. These are appropriate prayers, to be sure, when needed. And there is no doubt we will need to pray for supply frequently, for life surely throws us many challenges. This Christian life is meant to be robust; there is a toughness and a resilience we are meant to develop. We have not so much a sorrow side but a struggle side to this earth existence, and we are in for the fight of faith everyday.

But I think the joy side prevails (as I would with my name). I believe our more frequent prayers should be those of rejoicing and thanksgiving for the lovingkindness of our God. We need to notice, to be attentive. How giving he is—both with supply for our faith fight, and with those incredible gifts of wonder and love and beauty that grace our daily lives! Our focus is on the routine, so we miss much of the sheer goodness of life, as well as the zest of spirit. The more we cultivate the habit of praise and thanksgiving, the more we *realize* all we are blessed with.

When we are delighted with his gifts, we thank him. How important to go on to realize the incredible heart of love that does the giving. How does the Lord feel when we praise him for his very nature?

Moreover, it fills our hearts with delight *when we praise*. We experience a wonderful thing: we strongly sense both his presence and his delight. Of course, for the Holy Spirit is orchestrating, drawing out the music of our rejoicing, filling us with joy simultaneously. How rich, how alive we feel.

We are told over and over in Scripture to give thanks. More important than the fashion or wording of thanksgiving is the *doing* of it. Cultivating the habit of thanksgiving is like any other habit—it grows easier and more frequent as we practice. And each time we are blessed by the doing, and God is blessed by the receiving.

Whether in large ways with stirring music and magnificent choirs and robust singing together, in smaller groups that join together, or in individual ways—in singing along with our favorite CD, in dancing, in loud laughter or arm-waving, in the whispers of the heart to God for each small goodness—woven through and through the fabric of life as we live it, praise, worship, and thanksgiving *must* arise. Our God is worthy!

I am not sure how worship is separate from praise and thanksgiving. I only know that the better I know him, the more my adoration grows, and the more I must simply and directly tell him so, gladly and from my heart. I feel no duty to do so; I want to. Indeed I feel I must; I cannot contain it; it must be expressed; I overflow with it. And I sense his rejoicing when I do.

I could delineate many more ways we can give joy to God, but each would, I think, fit as a sub-division of one of these six categories. But don't mind trying to make a "fit"—just set your heart on pleasing him, and the Holy Spirit will gladly instruct you in it in the moments of your days.

CHAPTER TWENTY SIX

A FINAL WORD

How clear it has become to me then that I *can* continue to delight God even in my diminishment. These habits of delighting him can surely increase if I choose. I say I am willing but I often find I lack motivation. "I'm too tired," I think, and I am tired, it's true. Yet it may be that I am trying to barter with God. If he will give me more energy, I will then make every effort to please him. Nah, nah, nah! That won't do at all. Truly, without him, I can do nothing, especially in this matter of delighting him. I need cleansing from all my resistance. I also fail when I merely try dutifully, with just habit or lip service, and not from the fullness of my heart. This further exhausts me. I never want to have this delighting God devolve into *duty*! Therefore, I need frequent refueling if I am to delight him. I simply can't delight him unless I am filled with him and flowing in him.

Very often now I need to come to the secret place of quiet resting love with him, and let myself just *be* with him awhile. I need to find delight *in* him, knowing *he* will show me how to live as his child. I need to hear him tell me again that I *am* a delight to him just because I am his. He joys in me, he enjoys me, he is delighted with me, just as I am. So I rest down in it and just bask in his cherishing. After a time I either go to sleep, or, filled again, begin to sense a stirring within me. The *joy* of the *Lord* is my strength. Until I let him *joy* in me, I will not be motivated nor energized to delight him.

How do I so easily miss this simple and beautiful love relationship? I know the Lord's expectations of me will *always* match the energy he supplies. So I stay awhile, nestled in, letting the world hurl madly along at its fever pace, as I draw on Love that infuses me with a profound peace. The old song rises in me:

> O Love that will not let me go,
> I rest my weary soul in Thee;
> I give Thee back the life I owe,
> That in Thine ocean depths its flow
> May richer, fuller be.[5]

Then I stay awhile longer, just being there, sitting in serene silence, experiencing the union with him that defies words and even praise, the pinnacle of existence, the prelude to heaven.

A strange thought strikes me: out of diminishment, enlargement is born.

NOTES

1. Stuart Berg Flexner, ed. *Random House Dictionary of the English Language,* 2nd Ed. (New York: Random House, 1978).

2. Mark Buchanan, *The Rest of God, Restoring Soul by Restoring the Sabbath* (Nashville, TN: W. Publishing Group, 2006), pp. 36-37.

3. Charles Caldwell Ryrie, *The Ryrie Study Bible, New American Standard* (Chicago: Moody Publishers, 1978), p. 1337.

4. Malcolm Smith, *The Lost Secret of the New Covenant* (Tulsa, OK: Harrison House, 2002), p. 41.

5. Words by George Matheson, music by Albert L. Peace, "Oh Love That Will Not Let Me Go," *Hymns for the Family of God* (Nashville, TN: Paragon Associates, Inc., 1976), p. 404.

CPSIA information can be obtained at www.ICGtesting.com
Printed in the USA
LVOW06s1142140913

352381LV00001BA/29/P